The Black Archive #8

BLACK
ORCHID

By Ian Millsted

Published November 2016 by Obverse Books

Cover Design © Cody Schell

Text © Ian Millsted, 2016

Range Editor: Philip Purser-Hallard

Ian would like to thank:

Phil Purser-Hallard for his support. Thanks also to Ken Shinn for the loan of books, and moral support.

Also available

The Black Archive #1: Rose by Jon Arnold

The Black Archive #2: The Massacre by James Cooray Smith

The Black Archive #3: The Ambassadors of Death by LM Myles

The Black Archive #4: Dark Water / Death in Heaven by Philip Purser-Hallard

The Black Archive #5: Image of the Fendahl by Simon Bucher-Jones

The Black Archive #6: Ghost Light by Jonathan Dennis

The Black Archive #7: The Mind Robber by Andrew Hickey

Coming in 2017

The Black Archive #9: The God Complex by Paul Driscoll

The Black Archive #10: Scream of the Shalka by Jon Arnold

The Black Archive #11: The Evil of the Daleks by Simon Guerrier

The Black Archive #12: Pyramids of Mars by Kate Orman

The Black Archive #13: Human Nature / The Family of Blood by Naomi Jacobs and Philip Purser-Hallard

The Black Archive #14: The Daleks' Master Plan by Alan Stevens

For Elizabeth and Bethan

CONTENTS

OVERVIEW

Serial Title: *Black Orchid*

Writer: Terence Dudley

Director: Ron Jones

Original UK Transmission Dates: 1 March 1982 – 2 March 1982

Running Time: Episode 1: 24m 56s

Episode 2: 24m 41s

UK Viewing Figures: Episode 1: 9.9 million

Episode 2: 10.1 million

Regular cast: Peter Davison (The Doctor), Sarah Sutton (Nyssa / Ann), Janet Fielding (Tegan), Matthew Waterhouse (Adric)

Guest Cast: Barbara Murray (Lady Cranleigh), Moray Watson (Sir Robert Muir), Michael Cochrane (Lord Cranleigh), Brian Hawksley (Brewster), Timothy Block (Tanner), Ahmed Khalil (Latoni), Gareth Milne (The Unknown / George Cranleigh), Ivor Salter (Sergeant Markham), Andrew Tourell (Constable Cummings)

Antagonists: George Cranleigh, Lady Cranleigh

Novelisation: *Doctor Who: Black Orchid* by Terence Dudley. **The Target Doctor Who Library #113.**

Responses:

'The story of George Cranleigh need not have taken place in the 1920s, but the fact it did made both episodes true masterpieces.'

[David Richardson, 'Friend or Foe? *Black Orchid* Reviewed', *Skaro* vol 2 #5]

'It may sound sane and look pretty [...] but *Black Orchid* is as insubstantial as smoke.'

[Gary Gillatt, 'Black Orchid' (DVD review), *Doctor Who Magazine* #395]

SYNOPSIS

Episode 1

A case of mistaken identity at a rural railway station in 1925 allows the Doctor to join a charity cricket match convened by **Charles, Lord Cranleigh**, in which he distinguishes himself both as batsman and bowler. He and his friends **Nyssa**, **Tegan** and **Adric** accept Charles's invitation to a masked ball at his stately home. Everyone is surprised at how closely Nyssa resembles Charles's fiancée **Ann**. Ann was previously engaged to Charles's elder brother **George**, an explorer and botanist who before his disappearance discovered a rare South American black orchid.

At the ball, Nyssa and Ann tease the guests with their resemblance, while Tegan flirts with **Sir Robert Muir**, the Chief Constable of the county. Before dressing, the Doctor has accidentally become stuck in the secret passages which riddle the Hall, and his costume has been appropriated by a mysterious figure who has escaped captivity in a secret upper room. This man has already killed one of his minders, **Digby**, and the second – an indigenous Brazilian named **Latoni** – interrupts the party to inform Charles's mother, **Lady Cranleigh,** of his 'friend''s absence. Latoni and Lady Cranleigh find the Doctor wandering the corridors, and he shows them Digby's body which he has discovered in a cupboard.

Meanwhile Latoni's friend, in the Doctor's harlequin costume, turns a dance with one of the identical young women into an opportunity to drag her away into the house – throttling a footman, **James**, who comes to her aid.

Episode 2

Lady Cranleigh and Latoni find Ann unconscious in their disfigured prisoner's room. They free her and re-imprison him. Ann accuses the Doctor, now dressed in the harlequin costume, of James' murder. He protests his innocence, but a phone call reveals his earlier imposture, and Digby's body, which might have helped his case, has been removed. In desperation he reveals that he is a time-traveller, to general scepticism. Sir Robert has **Sergeant Markham** arrest him and his friends. The Doctor persuades Markham to detour via the train station to see some 'vital evidence', but the TARDIS is also gone.

At the Hall, Charles is appalled at his mother's behaviour in framing the Doctor for James's murder. He insists on telling Ann the truth about the culprit, which shocks her equally. Meanwhile, the man has escaped again, throttling Latoni and starting a fire. When the TARDIS – which had been removed to the police station, finally allowing the Doctor to prove the truth of his story – brings the Doctor, his friends, Sir Robert and Sergeant Markham back to the Hall, the mutilated man seizes Nyssa and carries her into the burning upper floors. Lady Cranleigh reveals that the abductor is her elder son, George, whose removal of their sacred orchid so offended an indigenous tribe that they tortured him, leaving him disfigured, mute and insane before his rescue by Latoni's people.

The Doctor and Charles confront George on the burning roof, and persuade him that Nyssa is not Ann. He lets her go, but when Charles tries to embrace him George recoils, and falls to his death. The Doctor and his friends stay for the funeral, and are thanked with their costumes and a copy of George's book, *Black Orchid*.

INTRODUCTION

For the 10 million viewers who watched *Black Orchid* (1982) when it was first broadcast there would have been much that was comfortingly familiar. The viewer is treated to steam trains and vintage cars and a murder in a country house. There is a cricket match being played. The period setting is 1925, which is only a decade or so away from the setting of the first three series of **All Creatures Great and Small** (1978-90) for which Peter Davison was still best known[1]. The regular cast portray four characters who have now spent some time together, and appear to be more at ease in each other's company, becoming an unorthodox, but functional, family unit. After the erratic behaviour of the Doctor in *Castrovalva* and the mental torture of Tegan in *Kinda* (both 1982) earlier in season 19, *Black Orchid* can be seen as 'an enjoyable mid-season break'[2].

At the same time there is much that is unfamiliar in *Black Orchid*. It is claimed to be the first purely historical story since *The Highlanders* (1966-67) some 15 years earlier when, it is safe to assume, the majority of those 10 million viewers were not watching the series. It is also a two-part story in a season and era when four-part stories were the norm. The last use of the structure of two 25-minute parts had been *The Sontaran Experiment* (1975), and the

---

[1] And only a decade later than that of the series **Wings** (1976-77), in which guest actor Michael Cochrane ha a regular starring role.
[2] Richardson, David, *Skaro* Volume 2 number 5, June 1982 as quoted in Howe, David J, and Stephen James Walker, *Doctor Who: The Television Companion*, p417.

format had only ever been used three times prior to *Black Orchid*[3]. There is also the unusual sight of the Doctor engaging in sport, specifically cricket – an organised team sport.

Black Orchid is something of a curio within season 19. Only the story it directly followed, *The Visitation* (1982), has a similar tonal quality, with the four time travellers resolving a puzzle in historical England. The crowd-pleasing *Earthshock* (1982) and the considered favourite *Kinda* have traditionally received the most critical attention of the seven stories shown that year. *Black Orchid* has risen and fallen over the years in terms of popularity with fans of the series, and has recently become a favoured target of 'The Watcher''s column in *Doctor Who Magazine*. It was producer John Nathan-Turner's favourite story of the season[4]. (Make of that what you will.)

The idea for *Black Orchid* came from the writer, Terence Dudley, whose credits for **Doctor Who** are clustered in the period from 1980 to 1983, but whose history with the series goes back to the very start. As stated in an interview in 1988:

> 'Before **Doctor Who** began, the original producer, Verity Lambert, asked me to write the very first story; but I was

---

[3] Originally in *The Edge of Destruction* (1964) and *The Rescue* (1965).

[4] Pixley, Andrew, 'Fact File', *Doctor Who Magazine* (DWM) 10th Anniversary Issue. Nathan-Turner was the producer of **Doctor Who** from 1980 until 1989.

heavily engaged elsewhere and it finished up with Tony Coburn.'[5]

In the same interview Dudley indicates that Barry Letts[6] had asked him to work on the series. This may have been as a director rather than a writer.

Dudley was an insider. He worked mainly in television and mainly for the BBC. He was a producer, director and writer. Sometimes he combined the roles. Other times, as in the case of **Doctor Who,** he performed them separately. He directed *Meglos* (1980), and wrote the scripts for *Four to Doomsday* (1982) and *The King's Demons* (1983) as well as the spinoff **K-9 and Company**: *A Girl's Best Friend* (1981) in addition to his work on *Black Orchid*. Among his many credits as producer are the well-regarded telefantasy series **Doomwatch** (1970-72) and **Survivors** (1975-77). Dudley had worked with John Nathan-Turner on **All Creatures Great and Small**, and Nathan-Turner clearly respected him. *Black Orchid* was first proposed to script editor Christopher H Bidmead[7] under the title 'The Beast'. Bidmead rejected the proposal, as it was not the type of scientifically-based SF story that he was trying to develop for the series[8]. After Bidmead's departure the story was proposed again, and commissioned by the incoming script editor, Eric Saward.

Black Orchid is, despite its short running time for a 20th-century **Doctor Who** story, leisurely paced. And yet, there is a surprising

---

[5] Walker, Stephen James, ed, *Volume Three: The Eighties*, pp29-30.
[6] **Doctor Who** producer from 1970 to 1975.
[7] Bidmead was script editor of **Doctor Who** from *The Leisure Hive* (1980) to *Logopolis* (1981).
[8] Pixley, 'Fact File'.

amount of hinterland. There are questions of identity, ideas about what makes a monster, references to colonialism and class structures and examinations of mental and physical disability. The relationship of both the Doctor and **Doctor Who** to all these will be examined.

Black Orchid is also the most 'crickety' of all **Doctor Who** stories, allowing us to ask what cricket tells us about the Doctor – especially, but not exclusively, his fifth incarnation.

CHAPTER 1: THE KNOWN

Black Orchid starts with a murder, but it is not a murder mystery in the classic whodunit style. We know from the start who the murderer is and can intuit most of the cause. Nor is the story structured in terms of 'How will they find out who the murderer is?' – the format used in the detective series **Columbo**, where the fascination is found in watching the detective pick away at the clues until all is revealed[9]. The structure is closer to that of a tragedy. Characters acting out of good intentions cause events to transpire that first obfuscate and then illuminate the truth. Along the way people are emotionally and physically hurt, and at least three people, and probably four, die.

So, *Black Orchid* is not a whodunit, but it is still a murder story. It also has a country house setting, which has long been a favourite location for murder stories, although not as common on television, in 1982, as our memories might have us believe.

The works of Agatha Christie have become such a mainstay of British television schedules that it is easy to assume that was always the case. However, Christie chose not to let most of her work be adapted for television during her lifetime, having been unimpressed with early adaptations. After she died in 1976 that situation changed. While there had been many successful film adaptations of Christie's work, such as *And Then There Were None*

---

[9] Helped by brilliant characterisation from Peter Falk. **Columbo** originally ran from 1971 to 1978, and was revived in 1989 with episodes continuing to be made until 2003.

(1945) and *Witness for the Prosecution* (1957)[10] it was the international commercial success of *Murder on the Orient Express* (1974) which showed what could be done with a good budget and strong cast. By 1980, television was ready to follow suit. ITV produced successful adaptations of *Why Didn't They Ask Evans?* (1980) and *The Seven Dials Mystery* (1981). Many more followed. By way of context for *Black Orchid*, *Why Didn't They Ask Evans?* has a plot that includes reference to sanatoria for the mentally ill, as well as a partial country house setting.

Although *Black Orchid* does not work as a murder mystery in story structure, it does have enough echoes of that style of television drama to suggest a conscious effort on the part of the writer and production team. Agatha Christie's detectives, whether professional or amateur, operate in the same world as the suspects, victims and perpetrators of the murders they investigate. Just as Poirot knows how to dress for dinner, the Doctor has always known how to mix with the upper classes[11].

We can look to another fictional detective character for a closer inspiration for *Black Orchid*. Dorothy L Sayers' novel *Murder Must Advertise* (1933) is clearly an influence on Terence Dudley. It features her amateur detective character, Lord Peter Wimsey, investigating a murder among the parallel worlds of some bright young things working in the advertising industry and another,

---

[10] The four Miss Marple films of the early 1960s are, arguably, more vehicles for Margaret Rutherford than adaptations of Christie novels. I love them all the same.
[11] As seen as early as *Marco Polo* (1964) and *The Romans* (1965) and many more thereafter.

mostly separate and distinct, set of bright young things seeking illegal drugs for their exclusive parties. The novel was adapted for television in 1973, less than nine years before *Black Orchid*[12].

Wimsey, like Poirot and Sherlock Holmes, has the quality also usually seen in the Doctor, of being the smartest person in the room. In *Murder Must Advertise* Wimsey is in control all the time, in a way regular viewers of **Doctor Who** also expect their protagonist to be. However, in this respect, Wimsey has the advantage over Davison's Doctor. As Paul Cornell has noted:

> 'the Harlequin costume echoes a similar costume once worn by Lord Peter Wimsey, the very opposite of the fifth Doctor. Wimsey conceals his abilities himself. The Doctor has them forcibly concealed by his appearance. He is, as Davison often says, an old man in a young body. This frustrates him. The confidence of experience is let down by appearances. He's not in charge, like Baker, because he thinks he should still automatically be, and doesn't see why he has to try so hard.'[13]

The harlequin costume Wimsey wears in the television version differs from the one in *Black Orchid* in that it does not hide the whole face. Wimsey uses the costume to establish one of two

---

[12] This was one of a number of adaptations of Sayers' novels broadcast in the early to mid-1970s starring Ian Carmichael as Lord Peter Wimsey. These mostly used a structure of four episodes of approximately 50 minutes each. At 53, Carmichael was a little old for Wimsey, who was supposed to be in his early 40s in the novel.
[13] Cornell, Paul, 'Black Orchid: Someone Somewhere (in Summertime)'. DWM Special Edition #1: *The Complete Fifth Doctor*.

disguises. He maintains those disguises consistently throughout the story. In contrast, Davison's Doctor would prefer to jettison his disguise and mingle as himself. It is true that Wimsey conceals his ability as a detective but he is never a silly ass. In his role as an advertising writer he demonstrates skill for the job[14]. Wimsey dons the role of the Harlequin in order to seduce his way to the information he needs to solve the case, and convinces as a romantic hunter-gatherer; more Errol Flynn than Pepé Le Pew. Davison's Doctor demonstrates his ability at cricket but the plot of *Black Orchid* never really allows him to demonstrate any detective skills or to take control of the action. Davison himself reflected on his role here.

> 'I never particularly liked *Black Orchid*, to tell you the truth, mainly because I seemed to spend a lot of time dressed up like an idiot... a clown, which I never liked. I don't know what it was that I didn't like about that story... Maybe it was just smacked too much of Noël Coward or something.'[15]

Like *Black Orchid*, *Murder Must Advertise* also involves a cricket match in the plot.

Another obvious influence on the plot of *Black Orchid* is Charlotte Bronte's *Jane Eyre* (1847). *Black Orchid* is not alone in this respect as Bronte's novel has been much imitated over the years. It is widely read and continuously in print. For those who absorb these stories through other media, the most recent television adaptation prior to the production of *Black Orchid* was the BBC version in

---

[14] Sayers worked in advertising herself.
[15] Briggs, Nick, 'Peter Davison – Dr Moo?' part 2, DWM #214.

1973. In addition, the 1970 US TV film had been screened in peak viewing time on BBC1 in 1980, and the 1943 film starring Orson Welles was well known. On the horizon was a new BBC adaptation, being produced by Barry Letts for the Sunday evening classic serial to be broadcast in 1983.

Jane Eyre has, at its centre, the story of a family with a secret in the form of a mentally injured relative. Through the eyes of the titular heroine we gradually discover the nature of that secret. She arrives at Thornfield Hall, which is owned by the absentee Mr Rochester and where she is to be employed as a governess to Rochester's ward. She soon becomes aware of something hidden in the attic of the grand house. That something is Bertha Antoinetta Mason, the wife of Rochester. Bertha is kept in a locked room where she is supervised round the clock by a paid servant. She married Rochester in Jamaica where he was working in the family business. In the novel Rochester later recounts how Bertha was already suffering from an inherited mental illness which gets progressively worse.

At a stroke, with the creation of Bertha Mason, Charlotte Bronte raises questions of class, race and feminism. If those issues are also present in *Black Orchid*, which will be examined below, then it is in part because of their presence in *Jane Eyre*. Jane Eyre, the character, occupies awkward positions in the class structure. She starts out as the poor relation of richer relatives, reliant on the kindness of others. That kindness is rarely offered. When she becomes a governess she is in a position above most other servants but not deemed to be on equal terms with her employer.

The question of race is implicit rather than explicit (and is examined more closely in Jean Rhys's prequel to *Jane Eyre*, *Wide Sargasso Sea* (1966)[16]). The Mason family are plantation owners in Jamaica. Although Bertha is described as 'tall, dark, and majestic'[17], it is to be assumed that she was white, as the plantation class were. Whether Bronte meant to imply that there was some Carribean ancestry in Bertha's family background is unclear. Rochester refers to her at one point as 'my Indian Messalina'[18] (with the use of the word 'Indian' indicating 'of the West Indies'), which, given that the reference to Messalina is a critical statement that Bertha was oversexed, is probably meant as a racial slur or insult rather than a geographical description. The treatment of both Bertha and Jane demonstrates Bronte's ability to illuminate the position and status of women at the time she lived (and beyond, frankly).

Black Orchid gives us a mad man in the attic instead of a mad woman, but in other ways the parallels are clear. Both are able to escape their guardian captors on more than one occasion. Both are seen by their families as someone, or something, of which to be ashamed. Both display homicidal tendencies. Both manage to set fire to the grand house which has served as their prison. In addition, both are examples of unrequited love – although that love had been returned, in each case, at some point in the past. Bertha

---

[16] *Wide Sargasso Sea* tells the story of Bertha (originally Antoinette) and her relationship with Rochester (not named in the novel but it is clear who it is meant to be). Rhys, herself of Creole heritage, writes Bertha as being of Creole ancestry and shows how this is one cause of the failure of the relationship with Rochester.
[17] Bronte, Charlotte, *Jane Eyre*, p343.
[18] Bronte, *Jane Eyre*, p350.

still loves Rochester, even though she tries to kill him. Rochester, by the time of the events in *Jane Eyre*, is repelled by Bertha and she knows it. Both are now inconveniently in the way of rich gentlemen wanting to marry someone. Bertha, if her existence is known, bars Rochester from marrying Jane Eyre. George Cranleigh's brother Charles is engaged to Ann, who was previously engaged to George but doesn't know he's still alive.

Bertha and Cranleigh both arrive in England from the Americas, bringing their madness with them. In Bertha's case, she has been born and brought up in Jamaica. That her condition is described as hereditary and therefore correlates to her family's lineage in the colonies is presumably intentional on Bronte's part. Cranleigh, in contrast, was an explorer in South America. All was fine until he went to that distant place. His madness has been inflicted on him during his time in the Orinoco basin[19]. He has, in turn, been brought close to the point of death and then saved, by different indigenous people of South America. (The seemingly contrary references to the Orinoco, which is mostly in Venezuela, and Cranleigh having been found in Brazil may suggest that he was exploring in the area of the Casiquiare canal – a natural rather than man-made feature – which links the tributaries of the Orinoco and the Amazon, and is mostly in Brazil.)

---

[19] One wonders if anyone in the Doctor *Who* production team knew that one of the potential writers for the series at this time, Andrew M Stephenson, was born, and had lived, in Venezuela. Stephenson was twice commissioned as far as scene breakdowns, for 'Farer Nohan' (March 1980) and 'The House That Ur-Cjak Built' (June 1982). (Howe, David J, Mark Stammers and Stephen James Walker, *Doctor Who: The Eighties*, pp5, 54.)

There is a long tradition of *Doctor Who* taking inspiration from literary and cinematic sources, and Terence Dudley is doing nothing for which he should be criticised in looking to *Murder Must Advertise* and, especially, *Jane Eyre* for a creative spark. Indeed, if you are going to borrow ideas then you can do far worse than Dorothy L Sayers and Charlotte Bronte.

The Philip Hinchcliffe/Robert Holmes[20] era of *Doctor Who* is especially remembered for strip-mining literary sources. Examples include *The Brain of Morbius*, which was inspired by Mary Shelley's novel *Frankenstein*, and *The Talons of Weng-Chiang*, which references Sherlock Holmes and Fu Manchu. It is also a highly regarded period of the series. But Hinchcliffe and Holmes were only being more obvious in following a tradition going back as far as *Planet of Giants* (1964), which owes something to both the book *The Shrinking Man* (1955) by Richard Matheson and even more the film adaptation, *The Incredible Shrinking Man* (1957). It is significant that these references nearly always have film or television adaptations with which the audience could be expected to be familiar.

While the ideas originate with the source novels, it is often the film versions which have the memetic influence that Robert Holmes and others were looking to use. *The Brain of Morbius* references in both story terms, and set designs, the Universal Studios horror films of the 1930s, including, but not limited to, their version of *Frankenstein* (1931). In some cases the film influences are direct

---

[20] Philip Hinchcliffe was producer of *Doctor Who* from 1974 to 1977 and Robert Holmes was script editor throughout that period.

and unaffected by literary sources. *The Romans* (1965) owes more to the version of history filtered through popular Hollywood epics such as *Quo Vadis* (1951) than to academic history texts. James Cooray Smith identifies that *The Massacre* (1966) is inspired in part by the novel *La Reine Margot* (1846) (and its 1954 film adaptation) and that *The Gunfighters* (1966) is most strongly influenced by the 1957 film *Gunfight at the OK Corral*[21].

The question then, is how Terence Dudley's inspiration leads to *Black Orchid* as it now exists, and how much of that development is due to Dudley, how much to the effect of being a **Doctor Who** story and how much to external factors such as budgetary restrictions.

---

[21] Cooray Smith, James, *The Black Archive #2: The Massacre* (2015), pp172-74.

CHAPTER 2: THE UNKNOWN

In the first episode of *Black Orchid* Gareth Milne, who plays George Cranleigh, is credited as 'The Unknown'. This was done in order to preserve the mystery of the identity of the killer, but it also serves to give those looking for a monster in the story a tag; a name. If someone was making Top Trump cards for **Doctor Who** in 1982, the one showing George Cranleigh would have had 'The Unknown' in big letters at the top of the card where others would have been labelled 'Cyberman' or 'Terileptil'.

There are three stages that most people go through in their relationship with *Frankenstein*. I will call these the Aware, the Pedant and the Smartarse.

The Aware is the stage we go through when we become familiar with *Frankenstein* as a cultural entity. This is usually not from the source novel to begin with. Most people in English-speaking countries have heard of *Frankenstein* but far fewer have read Mary Shelley's novel. In my own case I don't remember when I first heard the name but I would have been quite young. It may have been through reading the comic strip **Frankie Stein** in *Shiver and Shake* comic[22] or the reprint of Marvel Comics' **The Monster of Frankenstein** in the back of British Marvel weekly comic *Dracula*

---

[22] *Shiver and Shake* was a humorous comic published by IPC from 1973 to 1974. *Frankie Stein* had previously appeared in *Wham!* and was created by Ken Reid. There is no connection to the more recent character of the same name as featured in the **Monster High** books.

Lives[23]. The first film incarnation of *Frankenstein* I saw was almost certainly *Abbott and Costello meet Frankenstein* (1948). Most other film versions were only ever shown late at night, far past the bedtime of an eight- or nine-year old. The Frankenstein we know at this stage is a big lumbering monster, usually shown with bolts in his neck, stitch marks around the face and a dialogue rarely stretching beyond 'Urgh'.

At some stage we learn what happens in the actual story and we become the Pedant. This may come through reading the novel but more commonly is through watching film adaptations. I remember a Christmas edition of the *Radio Times* (and we were one of those families that only ever bought that edition) from 1975 that listed the showing of the 1973 American TV adaptation[24]. It showed Victor Frankenstein and the Monster as two separate entities. There were pictures of some of the cast and Victor Frankenstein (played by Leonard Whiting) didn't look anything like a monster to me. Nor did the Monster (Michael Sarazzin) look much like the guy from *Shiver and Shake*. I was further intrigued by other cast members. There was Jane Seymour from *Live and Let Die* (1973) and David McCallum who I'd seen in a **Man from U.N.C.L.E** film or two (1964-68) as well as **Colditz** (1972-74). And there was also, listed right at the bottom, Tom Baker, who'd recently taken over as the Doctor. It looked interesting but I didn't actually see the

---

[23] Originally published in the USA as *The Monster of Frankenstein* by writer Gary Friedrich and artist Mike Ploog. The version reprinted in *Dracula Lives* started with issue #6, by which time the comic and strip had both been renamed *The Frankenstein Monster*.
[24] Broadcast at 8:20pm on Saturday 27 December 1975 ('BBC Genome Project')

programme as we were, if I recall, visiting relatives and television was kept off on family visits (except for Auntie Joyce and she only ever watched ITV). A few years later I saw some of the Hammer films and the 1931 film with Boris Karloff as the Monster. Eventually I read the novel. I was fully prepared to inform anyone not in the know that 'Actually, you know, Frankenstein isn't the monster'. I could even point out that Abbott and Costello never actually meet Frankenstein.

The Smartarse stage is when we observe that, when Victor Frankenstein's motives and actions are examined, he might be a monster after all. He rejects his creation – his child – on the basis of its physical appearance and fails, subsequently and repeatedly, to take any responsibility for that which he has created. Meanwhile, we gradually become more sympathetic towards the creature that he creates. We understand his sense of abandonment and loneliness, which he articulates quite clearly. There is indeed more than one monster in *Frankenstein*, and don't we like to point that out! Perhaps Mary Shelley shows us the monster in all of us.

In *Black Orchid* the audience is likely to feel sympathy for George Cranleigh even though he kills two (or, probably, three) people. Our modern sensibilities may react to the fact that he is bound hand and foot. There is also a sense of injustice in that he is being deprived of the opportunity to be with the woman he loves. Above all, he is the victim of events beyond his control. As with Frankenstein's Monster there is a sense that, while George Cranleigh is a danger to human life, he is not the root cause of suffering in the story. This was observed as early as the immediate review in *Doctor Who Monthly* in June 1982:

'It did have a capable monster in the form of George Cranleigh, mutilated bodily and mentally by the torturous punishments of a South American tribe. The interesting thing about the marvellous make-up job done on Cranleigh was that it did not just inspire terror and revulsion. The make-up supervisor for this story, I would venture to say, learned a great deal from the success of *The Elephant Man* [1980]. As with John Hurt's brilliant portrayal of Merrick, so Gareth Milne, with the help of some expert make up, comes over not so much as an object of horror and fear but as a figure who inspired sympathy and pity for his disfigured condition.'[25]

Horror works in different ways. For Lady Cranleigh the horror is not what her son now looks like but in what happened to make him like that and in what might happen if he were to be discovered in his disfigured state. With regard to the former, the audience will have much sympathy with a mother who finds out that her son has been through the most horrific ordeal and that she is powerless to do anything to put it right. With regard to the latter there is likely to be much less sympathy. We can see that there is an ongoing sense of dread that Lady Cranleigh expects to experience every day for the rest of her life, but the viewer will not share her belief that it would be a dreadful thing should anyone find out that her son has been physically mutilated and mentally damaged. The actions she takes make her the closest thing to a villain as there is in *Black Orchid*.

---

[25] Review, *Doctor Who Monthly* #65.

The fear of mental illness was strong in Victorian society, and was reflected in contemporary literature. It is a classic case of fear of the unknown. Knowledge of the causes, and any treatments that might be successful, was limited. That which caused people to act, or react, in unpredictable ways was something to be feared or shunned.

Charlotte Bronte is somewhat ambivalent in her presentation of Bertha in *Jane Eyre*. There is an undoubted sense of injustice in the plight of a woman who has a marriage arranged by family who may not have her best intentions at heart. She is presented as a pathetic figure who deserves better than to be locked up and kept company by a woman, Grace Poole, who has enough flaws of her own. It should be noted that Bertha has the opportunity to harm or kill Jane but does not try to do so. It is the man she loves, but who has betrayed her, that is the target of her wrath. Among the women there is an odd sort of unknowing solidarity.

However, Bronte is less sympathetic when describing the moral decay into which Bertha's inherited madness has led her. Perhaps Bronte, as the daughter of a vicar, had a sense of moral rectitude. More likely, she had seen what alcoholism had done to her brother Branwell[26] and was willing to be judgmental about something which had caused genuine harm to her own family. Bronte was also aware of the Gothic tradition of literature from a generation

---

[26] In his relatively short life Branwell Bronte (1817-1848) suffered from alcoholism, drug addiction, indebtedness and an ultimately unhappy affair with his employer's wife. See Gerin, Winifred, 'Introduction' in Bronte, Anne, *The Tenant of Wildfell Hall*.

earlier. When Bertha attacks her own brother she sucks his blood[27], and Jane later compares her with 'the foul German spectre – the Vampyre'[28]. This is a reference to the short story of that name by John Polidori[29] as well as the folk legend, especially the version popular in German culture from which this spelling is derived and in which the vampiric figure is more often female. In doing so Bronte is identifying Bertha as a monster, even if she is a monster worthy of our sympathy and a victim of the way in which women could be treated, about which we should be angry.

Terence Dudley is following suit. George Cranleigh in his role as the Unknown is presented as a monster capable of taking human life but he is also deserving of sympathy.

That mental illness was something to cause fear as well as fascination can be seen in other contemporary works of literature. In *The Woman in White* (1859) Wilkie Collins tells the story of Anne Catherick and her commitment to a private mental asylum. Collins' biographer, Andrew Lycett notes that 'in this book, he gathered various strands – crime, lunacy, identity, inheritance, marriage and the sexes'[30]: in fact all the things we also find in *Black Orchid*. Collins was accused in his time of being a shocking or sensationalist writer, but he was also a writer who cared. Like his friend Charles Dickens, he was willing to use fiction to campaign against injustice.

---

[27] Bronte, *Jane Eyre*, p239.
[28] Bronte, *Jane Eyre*, p317.
[29] Polidori wrote the short story 'The Vampyre' after the same famous storytelling challenge that saw Mary Shelley produce *Frankenstein*.
[30] Lycett, Andrew, *Wilkie Collins: A Life of Sensation*, p192.

The Woman in White was written against the abuse of private mental institutions following several well-known cases such as that of Rosina Bulwer Lytton[31]. Collins also avoids using the mentally ill as monsters or villains, and instead creates a memorable villain in Count Fosco, whose motivation is money. *The Woman in White* was originally published in serialised form in *All The Year Round* magazine and was lapped up by the readers of the day[32].

East Lynne (1861) by Ellen Wood, writing as Mrs Henry Wood, was also originally a serial novel. Published from January to September 1861 in *The New Monthly Magazine* it tells the story of Lady Isobel Carlyle who, following her elopement, is abandoned, loses a child and is disfigured before becoming an unrecognised governess to her husband's new wife. As with George Cranleigh, the disfigurement becomes a plot device to allow someone to go unrecognised. The bigamous second marriage echoes Bronte but is also used in a more innocent, early-evening version in *Black Orchid*, where Ann Talbot is engaged to both Cranleigh brothers, albeit at different times. The themes of secret identity and class divisions also occur in *Black Orchid*.

That the victims in these novels are mostly women will have become apparent. Anthony Trollope tried to show that mental illness could affect men as well, in *He Knew He Was Right* (1869) which shows the decline into madness of Louis Trevelyan.

---

[31] Estranged and separated from her husband, Edward Bulwer-Lytton, Rosina publicly denounced Edward when he was standing for Parliament in 1858. She was restrained and held as being insane before being released after a public outcry.

[32] See Julian Simons' 'Introduction' to the Penguin edition (1974).

However, it should be noted that rather than being locked up in an attic or sent to an asylum, Trevelyan is allowed to retire to a quiet life in the country. While the illness may have been gender-blind, the responses of society were not.

Children could also be the focus of the literature of the locked away. In Frances Hodgson Burnett's *The Secret Garden* (1911) the 10- year old Mary Lennox, an orphan sent to live in Yorkshire after living in India all her life, hears a voice crying out from a part of Misselthwaite Manor. Her lonely exploration leads her to discover her own cousin who has hitherto been kept secret from her. Colin is kept from sight by the senior servants of the house while his own father largely lives away from the house and sees little of his own son. Colin is physically disabled rather than mentally ill, albeit not to the extent that he or others believe. *The Secret Garden* has a more optimistic outlook than the other novels mentioned above. This is partly a reflection of being intended for a children's audience but mostly reflects Burnett's philosophical approach when it came to understanding medical matters.

The madness of George Cranleigh is not the only depiction of mental illness in **Doctor Who**. There have been megalomaniacs such as Zaroff in *The Underwater Menace* (1967) or Harrison Chase in *The Seeds of Doom* (1976). Zaroff is implausible. There is no real explanation for his plans. Chase, however, is better written. He has a completely different worldview from all around him and acts consistently towards his objective. More subtle still is General Carrington in *The Ambassadors of Death* (1970), whose madness is a creeping paranoia derived from an inability to accept or process information about a changing world[33].

In contrast, George Cranleigh is not seeking to enforce his ideas on others. His illness is more debilitating, and causes him to do things we presume he would not have done before, but he is not a danger to the whole world. Like Zaroff and Chase, Cranleigh was once a brilliant man but his loss of sanity seems all the more tragic because we see the domestic situation he has come from and the people who love, or loved, him. A closer comparison is found in *Black Orchid*'s season 19 stablemate *Kinda*.

In *Kinda* we see Hindle, already in an advanced state of mental instability but not so far that we can't perceive the man he once was. The situation of Hindle and his colleagues among the Kinda people is a science fictional version of Cranleigh among the natives of South America. In both cases the visiting, or intruding, British expedition suffers through being in a place for which they are not remotely suited. The differences are that Cranleigh is, as far as we know, alone while Hindle is part of a larger, if rapidly diminishing, group – and in *Kinda* we see Hindle cured.

In *Black Orchid* we learn about Cranleigh's travels after the event and as reported by others. It seems to have been a journey to hell and back and one from which only the outer shell of the man remains, and even that in damaged form. On the other hand we also know that Cranleigh acquired enough information and experience to write his book, from which we can assume that the

---

[33] As detailed in LM Myles, *The Black Archive #3: The Ambassadors of Death* (2015), pp48-56.

expedition had satisfactory times before the final ordeal. The Earth expedition in *Kinda* is witnessed just after the tip-over point when things have clearly, for the visitors at least, reached the point of no return as they face madness and death. Most of the visitors have already disappeared, with only three remaining.

The expedition in *Kinda* is portrayed as archetypally British colonial. The casting of Richard Todd as Sanders is the most obvious short hand used by the production to that effect. Prior to becoming a major film star in the 1950s, Todd had spent part of his childhood in India where his father was in the army. Todd himself was an officer in the army in the Second World War, and in his acting career often played military or colonial figures as well as a range of swashbuckling heroes.

When Sanders slips into madness, Todd cleverly portrays him as devolving into a childlike state and manages to maintain that depiction remarkably consistently. Sanders is a dangerously stupid man who becomes mad as a result of events that occur to him when he travels into the world around him. Hindle is already unhinged before being presented with the gift, the Box of Jhana, which will force him into a whole new area of madness. Both Sanders and Hindle are military figures which Cranleigh is not, although he is clearly from the same class background from which the Sanders type is drawn. Perhaps Cranleigh in the Orinoco was more like Todd (as played by Nerys Hughes).

In *Kinda,* the Doctor enters the narrative at an earlier point in the story of the explorers than he does in *Black Orchid*. He acts as a random variable who is neither indigenous nor colonial intruder.

Complete disaster is averted but at a price. One of his own party, Tegan, suffers serious assault with lasting consequences.

Cranleigh is also a victim of a physical assault that renders him disfigured and deformed. Again, there is no shortage of examples of physical disfigurement in **Doctor Who.** Davros, first seen in *Genesis of the Daleks* (1975), is severely deformed from the norm for his race, the Kaleds. He is designed to be halfway between the humanoid Kaleds and the inhuman-looking Daleks. He is also, it has to be said, designed to be unpleasant to look at in order for that ugliness to act as shorthand for 'monster' and 'villain'. **Doctor Who** has not always fallen into this trap: Both *Galaxy 4* (1966) and *The Mutants* (1972) have as their main premise that assumptions should not be made on the basis of physical appearance. That which is different, the unknown, need not be feared just for that reason.

In the case of Davros there are reasons why he should be perceived as a threat by just about everybody else in the plot. Davros's desire for ultimate power of life and death over everything, and his willingness to do anything and sacrifice anyone in order to achieve that end, are what makes him a monster. It may be argued that the physical deformity Davros has experienced is what has made him think the way he does, but this is not shown. More recent episodes of **Doctor Who** have shown a willingness to explore Davros' past[34], and we may yet be shown more. George Cranleigh may look horrific but he is a victim rather than a monster. While Davros is a

---

[34] *The Magician's Apprentice / The Witch's Familiar* (2015).

Victor Frankenstein type of monster creating his own enduring monsters in the form of the Daleks.

Davros is all the more dangerous because of his greater competence and lack of humanity, whereas George Cranleigh is a monster only for those not looking past the superficial. He has something in common with the Phantom of the Opera[35] and Quasimodo, the Hunchback of Notre Dame[36] in being all too easily classified in the 'monster' category due to physical appearance alone, even though the personality inside suggests something quite different. Here again, **Doctor Who** is reflecting the mainstream awareness of those two characters rather than their original literary origins. The Phantom and the Hunchback both became part of the modern pantheon of monsters by virtue of their interpretations by Lon Chaney[37]. Chaney's films were silent, and therefore able to reach a truly international audience. Although they were marketed as sensationalist horror, Chaney himself imbued many of his characters with a sense of the real person

---

[35] *Le Fantome de l'Opera* (1910) by Gaston Leroux, in which a hideously disfigured man hides in the sewers beneath the Paris opera house. His love of music and the beautiful young singer Christine are both doomed to frustration.

[36] *Notre-Dame de Paris* (1831) by Victor Hugo. Quasimodo, who becomes the titular Hunchback of the novel's English title and its many film adaptations, is both physically and mentally disabled, but unlike George Cranleigh has been so since birth. The novel has an ensemble cast with, if anything, the cathedral itself being the main character. In the film adaptations it is always Quasimodo who is the main protagonist.

[37] In *The Phantom of the Opera* (1923) and *The Hunchback of Notre Dame* (1925).

underneath. As the child of deaf parents, Chaney knew from personal experience how people reacted to anything out of their usual; the other or unknown.

As well as being a skilled actor, Chaney's real genius was make-up. His Phantom, in particular, is still effective if viewed today. Like George Cranleigh, Chaney's monsters are first identified to us by way of their facial disfigurement. It's a trap we shouldn't really fall into, and Chaney and *Black Orchid* both use that prejudice of the audience as a starting point before taking us in another direction. After Chaney the Phantom, in particular, became a regular in the recurring cycles of horror films. In both cases the characters are known by the titles given to them, 'phantom' and 'hunchback', more than their true names. In most adaptations we gradually come to learn more about them, building sympathy and pathos as we reach the conclusion. This is a pattern followed in *Black Orchid*. The murderer is 'the Unknown', and then we learn enough about George Cranleigh that by the time of his death we have a sense of loss for the character.

Doctor Who has long been a monster show. It was not originally meant to be that way, but became known for its monsters as early as the second serial in 1963-64 when the Daleks first appeared. The monsters are one of things that people keep coming back for. They are what people go to the exhibitions for. We all love a good monster and over the years **Doctor Who** has delivered. It is also true that there have been some which have been ill-thought-out or poorly-designed (stand up Myrka[38] — then again, please don't).

---

[38] *Warriors of the Deep* (1984).

Having such a rich history of monsters gives the series the opportunity to regularly examine what we mean when we talk about monsters.

Is *Black Orchid* a monster-free story? Lady Cranleigh may be a villain but she is not a monster. She acts unwisely but does so, at least in part, out of love. George Cranleigh is no monster. If there is a monster in *Black Orchid* it is the society which seems to require the Cranleigh family to feel shame at what has happened to one of their number. In this respect the story would have worked better had it been set earlier than 1925, certainly prior to the First World War. By 1925 there were enough people around who had suffered emotional trauma and/or physical disfigurement that what happened to George Cranleigh would not have been as shocking as it might have been had the year been 1912 or thereabouts. If we overlook that detail, take the story on face value and accept the premise that Lady Cranleigh and Charles Cranleigh feel constrained by society and their place in it to such an extent that they have to bind and lock up George Cranleigh, then it is that society we should be seeing as the real horror.

Doctor Who has dealt in monstrous societies but usually in a science fiction setting in which the nature of the monstrosity is explicit from the beginning. In *The Happiness Patrol* (1988), for example, we see from the outset a society in which the freedom to dissent or feel melancholy – or feel anything – is denied. Although written as a satire on Thatcherite Britain, the artificial setting and exaggerated characterisation give us enough distance not to be as disturbed by that as we might be. If the same idea were used in a realistic near future setting, it would bring home to us how horrific that society is. We can apply the same principle to the society of

The Sun Makers (1977), where human life is devoid of any value other than monetary. Conversely, if we were presented with a story set on a future Earth colony in which any physical or mental abnormality were not publicly tolerated, we wouldn't automatically make the link to England in 1925 (or 1912). The greater likelihood is that the viewer would assume the inspiration was Nazi Germany.

We often fear the unknown, but the monster should be that which most disturbs and unsettles us – and that should be that which causes the most harm to the wider world around us and its occupants.

CHAPTER 3: CLASS, RACE AND COLONISATION

The Doctor is an aristocrat. He is part of a ruling class. Let's be clear about that. He may be a rebel lord and a reluctant ruler, but he is 'one of them'. The name 'Time Lord' is a bit of a giveaway. People are not identified as Lords unless there are other people who are not Lords, from which they feel a need to be distinguished.

The identification of the Doctor as part of a race called Time Lords did not happen until nearly six seasons had been broadcast. However, from the outset, the Doctor always seemed happier in the company of whoever made up the ruling class of whatever place the travellers found themselves. In *Marco Polo* (1964) he befriends Kublai Khan. In *The Keys of Marinus* (1964) he opts to travel straight on to the advanced civilisation while the others slum it in icy wastelands. (To be fair, that was a plot insert to allow William Hartnell a couple of weeks' holiday.) Even when aristocrats are out of favour in *The Reign of Terror* (1964), the Doctor manages to ingratiate himself with, and as one of, the new rulers of France. He talks with Robespierre on more or less equal terms.

The second Doctor is less inclined to prefer such company, although he has to play the part of a would-be dictator in *The Enemy of the World* (1967-68). The third Doctor reverts to type. When he is restricted to Earth he mixes freely with generals, senior diplomats and civil servants. He knows chaps from the club. For all his bluster against the establishment, especially in Malcolm Hulke's scripts, he is part of it. This carries on when he gets opportunities to travel to other planets. In *The Curse of Peladon* (1972) he poses as an ambassador at the court of the monarch of that planet. In *Frontier In Space* (1973) he hobnobs with Draconian royalty.

The fourth Doctor, for all his habitual rejections of the status quo, defaults to his aristocratic origins whenever the opportunity arises. Such opportunities are less common due to the nature of the stories and the move away from the UNIT connection; but note in *The Talons of Weng-Chiang* (1977) how, despite expressing a desire to see Little Titch, an entertainer favoured by the working class audiences of Victorian music halls, it is the affluent Professor Litefoot to whom he entrusts care of Leela. *The Deadly Assassin* (1976) revealed the Time Lords as a caste-based, aristocratic society which kept itself separate from other beings, the Shabogans, who live outside the citadel. Like Tony Benn rejecting the title of Lord Stansgate and the whole hereditary system from which it derived[39], the Doctor mocks this society, from which he sought exile, but is still very much part of it. He is a man entirely at

---

[39] Tony Benn was MP for Bristol South East from 1951 to 1983. In 1960 his father, Viscount Stansgate, died. The title was a hereditary peerage and Benn automatically became the second Viscount Stansgate with a seat in the House of Lords. This meant he would no longer be entitled to sit as an MP, and by 1960 it was inconceivable that a Prime Minister could hold that role while sitting in the House of Lords. Benn, both on principle and because he was an ambitious politician, wanted to continue as an MP. Benn fought a three-year campaign to change the law so that he could reject the peerage. The law was eventually changed in 1963 and Benn once more took his place in the House of Commons. It should be noted that his father only accepted a peerage in the first place because the Labour Party needed more members to represent the party in the House of Lords.

home with the gentlemanly activities of fishing or punting on the River Cam.

So, when Davison's Doctor cheerfully opts in to a day of country house cricket we should not be too surprised. The fifth Doctor was the first to have deliberately a gimmicky costume from the outset but the cricket outfit was still consistent with that of an Edwardian gentleman. Indeed, he is clearly meant to be a gentleman cricketer rather than a player. Steven Moffat[40] has observed the Doctor's status as follows.

> 'He's Robin Hood – he's a slumming-it toff. He believes he's a man of the people, but he still expects people to fetch him a cup of tea. Even Christopher Eccleston's Doctor... he tries to sound like a northern bloke, but you can tell that he's basically a prince. He just has the effortless presumption of one, and the occasional blindness. His heroism is that he rises above the limitations of the worldview into which he was born; to fight for a better universe for everyone. [...] There's a moment in *Hell Bent* [2015] I deeply regret cutting. The Doctor reveals that he's reassigned the High Council to the sewers, and Ohila remarks that only an aristocrat regards honest work as punishment. That's the Doctor all over, he knows that the aristocracy must be deposed, but even in bringing it about, he reveals that he will always be one of them.'[41]

---

[40] Producer and head writer on **Doctor Who** from 2010 to 2017, having previously written scripts for the series from 2005 onwards.
[41] Cook, Benjamin, 'The DWM Interview', DWM #500.

There are several reasons why this is the case. In story plotting terms it is easier to write a script where the main character has access to the people making the decisions. There is greater scope for dramatic tension if he can play off the rulers, and to do that he really needs to be in the same room as much as possible.

The BBC in 1963 was not yet looking to represent the working classes on television in significant numbers. Few of the production people were from secondary modern school backgrounds. The series reflected, more often than not, the sensibilities of the people making it.

It is also the case that the Doctor tends to assume a position of authority in whatever situation he finds himself on the basis of his abilities. He has, even if in an unconventional manner, leadership qualities. Others naturally look up to him.

The Doctor in *Black Orchid* expresses this aspect of his personality most clearly in the sporting and social situations, but in the main story strand, that of the discovery of the murderer, he is more passive. That is largely a fault of the script. Peter Davison is working hard with the material he is given. When required to wander aimlessly about the corridors, Davison does his best to give a sense that he is doing something other than being shuffled out of the plot for the time being.

Of the Doctor's companions, Nyssa, who is also of the ruling class of her own planet[42], mixes easily with the gentry and is also, of course, a physical double of Ann Talbot. Despite her alien origins,

---

[42] *The Keeper of Traken* (1981)

Nyssa has an understanding of the importance of ceremony and tradition. These are, if anything, more important on Traken than in 1920s England. She is able to place herself in this new class-based society with ease because she knows how such a society works. Aristocrats, it seems, are much the same anywhere in the universe.

Tegan is the most classless of the group but is relaxed in the company of Sir Robert and others. She comes from a background of working people, albeit ones who probably own the land and resources they have farmed[43]. When she first appears she is about to start her career as an air hostess. She has presumably studied and worked prior to this. In *Four to Doomsday* she demonstrates an impressive, if unlikely, ability to understand Aboriginal languages beyond anything she could have picked up other than by university level study. She is aspirational and willing to work to achieve her goals. Her choice of career suggests she wants to explore the world and is therefore open to new cultures and societies, as demonstrated in her enjoyment of the experiences offered in *Black Orchid*.

Adric is the one who is most out of place. He does not know how to conduct himself. The viewer is embarrassed on his behalf, although perhaps he deserves support for not conforming to the requirements of the class-based situation in which he finds himself. Like the Doctor he has moved from being part of a rigidly structured society to becoming an exile. His mathematical abilities had been recognised in such a way as to suggest he might have had

---

[43] In *Logopolis*, Aunt Vanessa refers to 'your father's farm', and Tegan says that her family have their own plane.

a bright future but he rejects that to become an outlaw[44]. On the basis of the information he has at the time it is a logical choice. The Starliner society is largely stagnant while the rest of the planet Alzarius may offer greater opportunities. The Starliner society from which Adric comes does at least appear to be more meritocratic than Traken. On the basis of his own experiences and logic, Adric has less reason than his companions to conform to the accepted behaviour of Cranleigh Hall.

The Doctor is also of independent means. He doesn't use money and shows little interest in currency of any kind. This disdain is something that only someone who has all they need can afford: those who have to work for a living are perpetually conscious of money and what they need it for. To be contemptuous of money is to dismiss the concerns of those without it. The TARDIS provides all that the Doctor needs. In this respect he is a wish-fulfilment figure rather than an audience identification character. We would like to be the Doctor and do the things he does, but we know we aren't and can't.

If we examine the record of the Doctor as rebel lord we will see that he is far more likely to lead or take part in a conflict of liberation from external forces – the equivalent of nationalist or independence struggles in the real world – than in class-based rebellions. Prior to *Black Orchid* there are at least 10 stories where the Doctor takes an active part in helping a society throw off rule by an occupying force of some kind or assist one race against

---

[44] *Full Circle* (1980).

another more belligerent one[45]. There are many more where he helps repel an alien invasion before such occupation can take place[46].

Some stories show societies where class and race (species) are inextricably linked, reflecting much of British colonial history. The Doctor's record in such stories is not clear cut. In *The Underwater Menace* he takes sides with the underclass against the rulers. The Fish People have been artificially altered, or created, to serve as workers. Essentially they are underwater plantation slaves. They are a new species designed to fulfil the role of an exploitable underclass. In *The Ark*, the position is more complicated. The underclass here, the Monoids, are clearly being exploited by the humans in the first two episodes. The suggestion that they are willing to accept that role (and how many times have we heard that argument in human history?) rings false. In the latter part of the

---

[45] *The Daleks* (1963-64), *The Dalek Invasion of Earth* (1964), *The Web Planet* (1965), *The Space Museum* (1965), *The Krotons* (1968-69), *The Sun Makers*, *The Power of Kroll* (1978-79), *Destiny of the Daleks* (1979), *The Horns of Nimon* (1979-80) and *State of Decay* (1980). There is room for argument here, and some people think there are other stories that should be added to the list on the basis of a broader definition of liberation struggles and what qualifies as the Doctor lending active support. I welcome correspondence.

[46] *The Tenth Planet* (1966), *The Moonbase* (1967), *The Abominable Snowmen* (1967), *The Web of Fear* (1968), *The Invasion* (1968-69), *The Seeds of Death* (1969), *Spearhead From Space* (1970), *Terror of the Autons* (1971), *The Sea Devils* (1972), *The Ark in Space* (1975), *Terror of the Zygons* (1975), *Pyramids of Mars* (1975), *The Android Invasion* (1975), *The Seeds of Doom* (1976), *Image of the Fendahl* (1977) and *The Invasion of Time* (1978).

story they have successfully overthrown their rulers and in turn subjugated the humans to slavery. The Doctor intervenes to help overthrow the Monoids, but this time encourages both races to work together in perfect harmony. *The Ark* is a clever and ambitious story which, unusually for the series, shows the long term consequences of the Doctor's actions. It does so using a unique story structure. However, if that story structure were to be extended to show a further jump forward would that perfect harmony still exist, or would one of the two races risen to the status of ruling class, exploiting the other? I wouldn't be too optimistic.

Another example of a 'race', if we stretch the term, being created in order to be exploited is shown in *The Robots of Death* (1977). The difference here is that the robots are artificial beings and we are therefore faced with the interesting moral question of whether it is more morally acceptable to enslave such beings. Further complexities are added by the main villain of the story having been raised by the robots, and also that one of the robots, D84, is the character for whom we have the most sympathy after the Doctor and Leela. The Doctor intervenes to save human life and therefore places himself in opposition to the idea of the robot underclass overthrowing their rulers, but he does so more to oppose the human who would lead them in that revolution rather than because the human society here is one worth preserving for its own sake.

In *Doctor Who and the Silurians* (1970) the Doctor is clearly sympathetic to the position of the Silurians. Their case is a good one. They were the first sentient rulers of the planet. They are not invading aliens. They were here all along, and they were here first.

Some of the Silurians would conquer the human race and use them as slaves while others would aim for peaceful co-existence. It does not fit the pattern of either class revolution or nationalistic liberation struggle. It is closer to being a child-friendly take on events in the Middle East, as much in the news in 1970 as today. It is possible to have either a pro-Palestinian or pro-Israel reading of the story. The Silurians could be the Palestinian people wondering how their land got taken away from them, or they could be the Jewish Israelis, returned after a 'very long time' to find other people living where they once lived, but determined to make it their own again.

It's also a story where the Doctor loses. He wants to make peace but fails utterly. In the sister story *The Sea Devils* (1972) it is the Master, rather than the Doctor, who is actively supporting the revolutionaries. Again this is nationalistic in nature rather than class-based, and it should be observed that the Master acts as he does for his own reasons. He has no interest at all in any moral claims that the Sea Devils might have. He is using them as proxies to attack his enemies: the Doctor and the human race.

Only in *The Savages* is the Doctor truly instrumental in helping an underclass overthrow an exploiting ruling class, and even then he leaves Steven Taylor to 'guide' them in case they are not yet ready to rule themselves (reflecting an attitude expressed frequently in the 1950s and 60s, as the United Kingdom negotiated independence settlements with colonies around the world).

In *The Monster of Peladon*, the Doctor helps the ruling hereditary monarch come to terms with representatives of the workers in order to avoid a total rebellion. If, as Steven Moffat suggests, the

Doctor is Robin Hood, then he is more likely to be the Robin Hood who leads Saxons fighting against Norman rulers than the Robin Hood who leads peasants against their noble rulers. The Doctor is a campaigner against injustice, but not a true revolutionary. In *Black Orchid* this manifests in the Doctor's concern for the dead servant Digby. While Lady Cranleigh would prefer the dead bodies to quietly disappear, the Doctor wants the authorities to investigate.

The Doctor is not the only Lord in *Black Orchid*. There are two Lords Cranleigh, but only one can be true. George is the elder son and had presumably already inherited the title as Lord Cranleigh before he left for South America. With George declared legally dead (and we wonder how Lady Cranleigh managed to do that), Charles has succeeded to the title[47]. This is a fraudulent status until George Cranleigh's tragic death at the end of the story. In a story with multiple doubles (of which more later), it is not inappropriate to have two claimants to the title 'Lord Cranleigh'.

The class structure, as shown in *Black Orchid*, also highlights the racial attitudes of the period. Latoni is a chief among his own people, but he is clearly not treated as an equal by the Cranleighs. It can be argued that Latoni is there to take care of George Cranleigh and should therefore not be seen too much in case the purpose of his residence is discovered. Perhaps. The day of the events in the story is not a typical one as there are many guests

---

[47] Terence Dudley's novelisation of the story gives more detail than on screen: specifically, George was the ninth Marquess of Cranleigh and has been succeeded by Charles as the 10th Marquess. The novelisation also gives the family name, without title, as Beauchamp (Dudley, Terence, *Black Orchid* (1986) pp11, 43).

staying at the house, but the reactions of those who do see Latoni suggest that only Lady Cranleigh knows who he is. This implies that he has not been a dinner guest when Ann Talbot or Sir Robert have been hosted on more normal days. The likelihood is that he did not take his meals with the servants either but, like Jane Eyre, occupies a social position that is neither one thing nor the other. Jane Eyre eats with the housekeeper. Latoni presumably eats with George Cranleigh.

Latoni's racial difference is indicated most obviously by his physical appearance. He has, according to the customs of his people, by use of artificial means, developed an extended lower lip. This is cleverly done. The physical deformity of Latoni, as perceived by everyone else in the story, foreshadows the appearance of the Unknown. We are presented with something we have to process. Latoni is a dignified character, albeit one who has become part of the imprisonment of his friend George Cranleigh. Lady Cranleigh treats him with respect if not as a social equal. Most of the guests at the fancy dress party, on seeing Latoni, assume he is in fancy dress himself. The Doctor refers to him as 'the Indian'.

It is the physical difference of Latoni that is relevant in *Black Orchid* rather than his skin colour. The racial attitudes of the rest of the cast are implied rather than explicit. No one is obviously hostile to Latoni but nor is anyone seen to go over and chat to him or ask him to dance. He is there to provide a link back to South America and to the tragic events relating to George Cranleigh. In that respect, although he is a friend and protector of George, he is also a physical reminder of the dangers of the unexplored rainforest. To use racial difference to move the story forward helps the writer to avoid extra exposition, but it also reinforces attitudes to race which encourages stereotypes. The viewer may intuit the former friendship between Latoni and George Cranleigh as one of equals where race was irrelevant, but it would have been interesting to see that presented somehow.

Some of these ideas were also present in Dudley's previous script for **Doctor Who**, *Four to Doomsday*. Here too, he uses race as a kind of dramatic shorthand. The four representatives of human cultures are all, essentially, stereotypes. This is exemplified most clearly in the dance pageant that they are required to perform for the Urbankans. Dudley deserves some credit for writing about a race of advanced aliens who have visited Earth at different points without trying to conquer and occupy, but what they are doing instead, collecting species of different human civilisations, is little better. This mirrors what George Cranleigh was doing in the Orinoco. He was not trying to take over territory for the British Empire but he was, it seems, going in with the aim of finding and taking something to which he had no entitlement. What the Urbankans and Cranleigh are both doing is a form of cultural appropriation. So too, arguably, is Dudley when using stereotypes to represent the cultures selected. Perhaps we, the audience, are also guilty of cultural appropriation by accepting all this for the purposes of our own entertainment without asking too many questions.

The track record of race in **Doctor Who** is a varied one. In terms of representation of non-white actors in the series it is largely in line with BBC drama of the times in which it was being made[48]. This means that for much of the time up to the mid-1980s it failed to give an indication of the demographics of British culture. The only way that the ITV science fiction series **The Tomorrow People** (1973 to 1979)[49] compares favourably to **Doctor Who** is in terms of the presentation of racial diversity. Of the eight tomorrow people featured in the original run of the series two were Black, one Asian and one Traveller. **Doctor Who** had to wait until 2007 for the first full-time non-white companion (although it should be noted that the *Doctor Who Magazine* comic strip had a non-white companion in 1980, and the New Adventures series of novels had a non-white companion in Roz Forrester from 1995. The spinoff series **The Sarah Jane Adventures** had an ethnically diverse cast from the outset in 2006).

In terms of how race is portrayed in the narrative of the series, **Doctor Who** has a better record than some of avoiding using non-white characters as victims but it is not until the late 1980s that there are significant non-white characters with agency or authority. Brigadier Winifred Bambera in *Battlefield* is one of a number of examples from that era of the series. This represented progress but

---

[48] Ahmed Khalil, who plays Latoni, is an Asian actor. It would be unusual in the 21st century to cast an actor of his background as a native South American, but in 1982 that was progress from the previous pattern of using make-up to let white actors play any role, as happened in, for example, *The Talons of Weng-Chiang*.

[49] **The Tomorrow People** ran on ITV and was produced by Thames Television for the weekday children's television hour. It was never really meant to be ITV's answer to **Doctor Who**.

from a very low base. The situation improves dramatically from 2005 onwards.

Latoni apart, the characters shown in *Black Orchid* are part of a society which is still a colonial power. The British Empire was still significant in 1925. If anything, due to the extra territory (Tanganyika, Iraq, Jordan, Palestine etc) mandated to British 'protection' after the First World War, the British Empire was larger than ever. It would have been generally accepted among the guests at a country house party that the British ruled over other peoples and places, at least partly because they **were** other peoples. This idea is not challenged in *Black Orchid*. There is no criticism of George Cranleigh for travelling to, and intruding into, another culture with the express intention of finding and bringing back the black orchid. To be the great white explorer is not portrayed negatively. After all, is that not what the Doctor is himself?

Colonialism is present in much of **Doctor Who** in the form of human expansion into a future interstellar empire of some kind. As early as *The Sensorites* (1964) we see a spaceship of white British explorers travelling to other stars and planets. There are notable exceptions, such as the international make-up of the cast in *The Moonbase* (1967), but generally the assumption presented in **Doctor Who,** as in much Western space fiction, is that humans will colonise the stars and the colonists will be white Europeans and North Americans. It is also assumed, again with notable exceptions such as *The Mutants*, that such colonisation will be a good, or at least a perfectly acceptable, thing. Even if the explorers and would-be-colonists frequently face great peril and die in large numbers, their presence in such places is largely unquestioned by the Doctor. After all, it is his own race's seeming isolationism that seems to have been one of the causes of his leaving Gallifrey. The Monk, The Master, The War Lord and others have turned renegade for similar reasons. The Doctor likes to differentiate himself in that he seeks to help others rather than seeking power for himself, but in the end he interferes as much as anyone in the lives of others.

George Cranleigh was only doing what the Doctor himself would do. Substitute the blue jewel of Metebelis 3[50] for the black orchid. Is there really a significant difference?

---

[50] *The Green Death* (1973).

CHAPTER 4: CRICKET

If class and colonialism are an accepted part of the world for the characters in *Black Orchid*, then cricket is the sport that binds those things together.

Even up to the present day cricket has an image for many people as something quirky and old-fashioned, which of course is how many people still think of 20th-century **Doctor Who.** This goes against the facts. Cricket is a massively popular global sport followed by millions of people all around the world, and has embraced technology to ensure the best decisions possible, in a way that puts many other sports to shame. It is, however, a game still linked to the former British Empire. The main countries where the game is played as a mass participation sport are all former colonies and dominions of the United Kingdom: specifically Australia, India, Pakistan, Sri Lanka, Bangladesh, New Zealand, South Africa and the island states that make up the West Indies team[51]. Although the sport has gained popularity in recent years in countries as diverse as Afghanistan and the Netherlands, if someone wants to make a living playing the sport they would need to go to England or one of the countries listed above. Of course, in places like Australia and the West Indies cricket provided an outlet for anyone wanting to stick it to their former colonial masters, and over the years many have done that in style.

---

[51] Including the non-island state of Guyana. Prior to independence it was quite usual for white players to retain positions of authority, such as captain, in a team mostly made up of black players, even where the white player did not merit a place on ability.

Cricket holds a unique place in **Doctor Who.** The series does not 'do' sport very often. Prior to *The Lodger*[52] (2011) few sports other than cricket entered the narrative. There was the fourth Doctor's desire in *The Androids of Tara* (1978) and *The Two Doctors* (1985) to go fly-fishing, which, like cricket, is an activity which tallies in the public consciousness as something an eccentric gentleman of the type the Doctor is usually portrayed would be likely to do. *Black Orchid* is the most 'crickety' of **Doctor Who** stories, but it is not the first or only one to reference the game. It is used in *Black Orchid* for narrative purposes even if it is allotted a generous amount of screen time in such a short story. Terence Dudley explained his own purpose clearly.

> 'Right from the beginning, **Doctor Who** has been, for me, what Sydney Newman asked for, an Edwardian gentleman. Cricket is a metaphor for this. I used, when younger, to play well. I captained the First XI at school. I love it and all the game implies, and I'm very, very sad to see the way the game's going... gentlemen are on their way out, too.'[53]

It is hard to conceive of any incarnation of the Doctor save that played by Matt Smith playing football with any degree of authenticity. It is, however, quite plausible that any of the Doctors could turn out for a game of cricket, even Hartnell's first Doctor. Cricket is a far more physically demanding game than it looks to the novice eye, but it does also work in such a way that someone sufficiently skilled in a certain aspect of the game could hold a place

---

[52] In which the 11th Doctor displays his abilities at football, courtesy of Matt Smith, who was a talented youth player.
[53] Walker, *Volume Three: The Eighties* p41.

in the team even if their general athleticism is below that of the others. However in 'Volcano' (*The Daleks' Master Plan* episode 8, 1966), the Doctor seems to be unaware of the game when the TARDIS lands at the Oval cricket ground during a test match between England and Australia[54].

At some point the Doctor obviously gained more knowledge of the game. The first mention in the series of the Doctor actually playing cricket is in *The Ribos Operation*[55] when he make reference to being a 'leg spinner' while miming a delivery. Leg spin is considered by aficionados of the game to be one of the most skilful arts. It is a way of bowling the ball, achieving spin by a combination of a set grip on the ball and a sharp twist of the wrist as the ball is delivered. Executed well it results in a larger degree of spin away from the expected line of delivery of a straight ball, which in turn makes it more difficult for the batsman to predict where the ball will be when it arrives. Practitioners of this method of bowling have included Australians Richie Benaud and Shane Warne. Given the ability of Tom Baker's Doctor to deliver unexpected dialogue, it would be entirely in keeping for him to be able to bowl such a delivery. Of course, he could just be trying to bamboozle his new and better-qualified Gallifreyan companion by talking about something of which he is sure she would know less than he.

---

[54] For completeness's sake it is noted that in the comic strip story *Egyptian Escapade* in *TV Comic* #820 (2 September 1967), the second Doctor lands the TARDIS in the middle of a cricket match in Egypt and recognises the game.

[55] Written by Robert Holmes and script edited by Anthony Read.

The next mention is in *The Horns of Nimon*[56] where the Doctor makes the aside 'with a talent like mine I might have been a great slow bowler'. He also acts out a delivery action again.

Around this time there were several attempts to bring to the screen a story which would have placed even more emphasis on cricket, but in a more subversive way. Douglas Adams had submitted two story ideas to the **Doctor Who** production office before being commissioned to write *The Pirate Planet* (1978). The second of these was 'The Krikketmen', which was rejected as being too silly. He later tried, with support from Tom Baker, to get interest in 'The Krikketmen' as a film project.[57] Both versions, and a possible third version for television in 1979, involved cricket-playing robots. The idea of robots from another planet playing cricket subverts the audience's expectations of what we expect from invading hordes and possibly makes us question the nature of cricket as a game invented in England (we presume; the origins of the game are complex). However, we will never truly know if this would have worked on screen. We do, though, have an idea of the philosophical ideas Adams was looking at, as he eventually used the basic idea as part of his novel *Life, the Universe and Everything* (1982), the third in his **Hitch-Hikers Guide to the Galaxy** series. Here, Adams shows how human beings have developed a game which mirrors an event from an alien culture. Unfortunately the event itself was a tragedy of epic proportions which the game of cricket seems to be mimicking with somewhat bad taste.

---

[56] Written by Anthony Read and script edited by Douglas Adams.
[57] Simpson, MJ, *Hitchhiker: A Biography of Douglas Adams*.

So, if the fourth Doctor was a spin bowler, specifically a leg spin bowler, then why does the fifth Doctor play for Lord Cranleigh's XI as a pace bowler? It is possible that different regenerations play different sports in different ways. Where leg spin bowling suited the fourth Doctor's quirky and individualistic personality, the fifth Doctor has a more dashing and open personality which manifests itself in cricketing terms as trying to outplay the opposition physically as well as mentally.

In Terence Dudley's *Four to Doomsday*, reference is made to bowling a 'chinaman'[58]. A chinaman in cricket is a leg spin delivery, but specifically one bowled by a left-arm bowler. The fifth Doctor never exhibits left-handedness, or any particular degree ambidexterity. Otherwise, the same principle applies. The type of cricket skills being referred to are unusual, quirky and requiring special ability – all in keeping with the ongoing personality of the Doctor.

But is the fifth Doctor really a fast bowler in *Black Orchid?*

Let's first examine that claim. As Paul Cornell observes, 'he tells Lord Cranleigh that he's a fast bowler (when he's actually just medium pace) with nose-up arrogance'[59]. This is a limitation of making television. Genuine fast bowlers, those able to bowl in excess of 90 miles per hour on a regular basis, are very rare. There are only ever a handful in the international game. To expect an

---

[58] In a nice touch, this story also shows Davison's Doctor using a cricket ball and some basic applied science to get himself out of a tricky spot.
[59] Cornell, 'Black Orchid'.

actor, even one with some experience of the game, to convince as a real fast bowler without the aid of trick camerawork not available to the production team at the time, is asking the impossible. They could have amended the script, but the Doctor arriving and announcing himself as a journeyman medium pacer would sound ridiculous.

Were fast bowlers not as quick in the 1920s as they are today and is the Doctor actually bowling at a pace which would have passed for quick at the time? This doesn't seem likely. While film footage of fast bowlers of the past appears to make them look slower, those who saw such bowlers over a long period of time state that those films do not convey the truth. There were umpires around in the 1970s who were players in the 1920s, and they said that Harold Larwood, the feared English fast bowler of the infamous Bodyline series, was as fast as the likes of Jeff Thomson or Andy Roberts. (Actually Larwood is one bowler who still looks pretty quick in the old newsreel footage.)

Peter Davison has spoken about this himself:

> 'The cricket scenes were done in one afternoon, and it was pouring with rain. It was absolutely pouring! The thing with filming is that you can't see the rain unless it's very, very heavy […] and that's my excuse for my bad play! I know I look very good – well, I look alright – but that was only after they cut out all the times the ball fell out of my hand when I was running up to bowl! […] But my one claim to fame was captured on film by accident. The cameraman, who wasn't a cricketer, was told to frame-up on me running up to bowl, so that they could use it as a shot of me running up and

delivering the ball; nothing else was meant to be in shot. [...] So I ran up to bowl, and I bowled it – and I bowled him out! [...] So it's there, and if you look carefully you'll see that it's no trick shot. I run up to bowl, bowl the ball and bowl him out. I never did it again! But it was fun to do, yes. I felt almost like a good player.' [60]

Cricket is a difficult game to do justice to in drama. It is interesting to note how many really good films there have been about baseball: *Eight Men Out* (1988), *Field of Dreams* (1989), *Bull Durham* (1988), *Pride of the Yankees* (1942), *The Stratton Story* (1949), *The Natural* (1984), *A League of Their Own* (1992), *Cobb* (1994) and others. In contrast there are relatively few films about cricket at all, regardless of quality. The makers of *The Final Test* (1953) made the shrewd move of using professional cricketers for the cricket scenes and actors for the dramatic scenes, with only minimal crossover. That apart, there is *Lagaan* (2001) and *Wondrous Oblivion* (2003). Less successful are *Playing Away* (1987), *Iqbal* (2005) and *Hansie* (2008) [61].

Baseball, like boxing, lends itself to dramatic representation on film because of its gladiatorial nature: it is one person against another. Even though it is a team sport, the camera only really needs to focus on the pitcher and the batsman to get the essence of what is going on. Cricket could be shown the same way, but most directors

---

[60] Walker, *Volume Three: The Eighties* p64-65.
[61] My personal favourite cricket scene in any film is the one in *The Dish* (2000) where two Australian lads are playing in the bowl of a large satellite dish. Brilliant idea; no need to run and field the ball as it will always come rolling back to the middle.

don't put the camera in the right place to capture the intensity of the action. The cricket scenes in *Black Orchid* are better filmed than those in many television dramas with higher budgets, and the cast, extras, director and production team are to be commended on what they managed in a half day filming in steady rain.

As an aside, I remember listening to Fred Trueman talk on **Test Match Special** about playing in a charity match with Peter Davison. Trueman, a truly great player for Yorkshire and England and a genuine fast bowler, went on to become something of a professional curmudgeon on the radio commentaries on cricket. He was frequently dismissive of the abilities of the players he watched, but I vividly remember him saying on air during a radio commentary from 1982 or 1983 that 'Doctor Who' was a good player. Unsupported memory, however, is notoriously unreliable.

Even though the cricket match gets a generous share of the running time of this story, Terence Dudley chose to add even more detail in his novelisation. This is mostly in the form of Tegan trying to explain the game to Nyssa and Adric, who are bewildered and disinterested respectively[62]. It is quite funny in a predictable way, playing on the old cliché of cricket being incomprehensible to foreigners, or in this case, aliens. I would argue that cricket is not really as complicated as all that. The basics of the game can be explained in a few minutes to an interested ten year old anywhere from Perth to Durham or Karachi to Soweto, to the extent that if given a bat and ball they will start playing a recognisable form of

---

[62] Dudley, *Black Orchid*, pp20-23.

the game. It is the terminology that makes it sound more complicated.

(And if Nyssa and Adric don't get it then they are not alone. Sir Robert, in the novelisation, tries to claim that the Doctor's innings counts as a record in first-class cricket – the name given to the professional level of the game, even if played by amateurs – because Lord Cranleigh's XI are playing against a minor county team. It would have meant nothing of the kind. The matches that would be classified as first-class are designated so by the authorities – the MCC[63] at the time – before they are played. The match in *Black Orchid* would have been several rungs down from first-class.)

Cricket both reflects and undermines the class structure of England. This was certainly true in 1925. All the players in *Black Orchid* are amateurs. The minor counties team would have played in their spare time, and we assume that Lord Cranleigh's XI is made up of his friends who have time to travel around doing this kind of thing. At the top level, cricket in 1925 was divided into amateurs and professionals, but the word 'amateur' was used to describe someone who chose not to be paid because they didn't need the money. They were full-time players. Cricket was what they did. They just had sufficient money or income by private means that they didn't need to be paid.

In contrast, the professionals of the era like Harold Larwood made a profession of cricket as an alternative to working in a coal mine. He was paid by Nottinghamshire County Cricket Club as an

---

[63] Marylebone Cricket Club.

employee. Once the game starts, however, all play on an equal basis. Larwood was given free rein to bowl as fast as he could at any batsman, be they amateur or professional. The distinctions were not always clear cut. WG Grace (who is referred to in *Black Orchid* as 'the master', a joke which seems laboured), maintained an amateur status so that he could call himself a gentleman, but nearly always played for money in reality. He was not paid a wage by his club, but often performed for appearance money, collected generous expenses and traded on his huge fame by charging people if they wanted him to pose for photographs. Grace was actually a doctor as well, a profession which also allowed himself to comport himself as a gentleman while still collecting money. Perhaps a better joke could have been made about WG being 'the doctor': Sir Robert tries when he refers to him as 'the other doctor'. In reality, it was another cricketer, Jack Hobbs, who was still playing in 1925, who was sometimes given the name 'the master'.

The Doctor plays cricket here as a gentleman amateur, as would, we presume, 'Smutty' Thomas, the cricketing medic whom the Doctor replaces for this match. It is yet another way in which we see the Doctor as aristocrat. We are used to the Doctor being brilliant without seeming to try, but we do know, when we think about it, that he has trained in the field of science. He has studied at the Time Lord academy as well as, if we believe his occasional name dropping, other institutions, including some on Earth. The brilliance is actually a result of some graft in the past as well as natural talent. But with the cricket he performs match-winning feats without any indication that he has ever trained to do so.

He is a dilettante. It is something of a disservice to the professionals like Larwood, a true great of the game, that this person of independent means can swan into a game and be effortlessly superior to all around him. It is colonial Britain's view of how things work. Similarly, the description in the novelisation, of Smutty being someone who could have played cricket for England had he not dedicated himself to medicine[64], smacks of the implied class structure agenda behind the long-perpetuated nonsense that there was something more worthy about amateur sports. The enforced protection of an amateur status in sports like cricket, tennis and athletics late into the 20th century was another way of stopping people who had to work for a living from being able to rise to the top. If someone is talented enough to earn fame and fortune at something, they should not be barred from doing so by people who want to preserve that opportunity for a self-selecting few.

After *Black Orchid*, television **Doctor Who** largely got cricket out of its system (until *Human Nature* in 2007). Writers of the character in other media still remembered though. Paul Cornell has gone on record about his love for the game, so it should be no surprise that his **Doctor Who** novels have made references to it - see, for example, *Goth Opera* (1994) which features the Fifth Doctor, Nyssa and Tegan and a charity cricket match in Tasmania in 1993. There are identifiable cameos for Australian batsman David Boon and bowler Merv Hughes[65]. The Doctor gets out for 90 runs[66]. Then there is the comic strip story *Nature of the Beast* (1986), in which

---

[64] Dudley, *Black Orchid*, p12.
[65] Boon and Hughes were both larger-than-life characters within the highly successful Australian national team of the 1990s.
[66] Cornell, Paul, *Goth Opera* (1994), p24.

the Sixth Doctor draws on his bowling skills to get himself out of a tight spot. More recently there was a flashback sequence in *The Forgotten* #3[67] (2008) showing the Doctor playing cricket while the watching Tegan tells Turlough that Australia 'beat England, Oh, I don't know, every time we play them.' (That statement was less true in the time that Tegan came from than in the era since. If Tegan is from 1980 then in the two most recent series between England and Australia she could have followed, in 1977 and 1978-79, England had won[68].)

The Doctor as cricketer is at the same time the unconventional adventurer and a figure of establishment orthodoxy. The time setting for the story accounts for that in part. I've played cricket at a low level for various works teams, church teams and village teams and it is, these days, quite egalitarian. I've yet to be asked to play country house cricket[69]. Like the fifth Doctor, I liked to think of myself as a fast bowler but the reality was, I fear, quite different.

---

[67] Written by Tony Lee and published by IDW Publishing.
[68] In the case of the 1978-79, series the Australian team was largely a second XI as most of what would have been the first team were playing in a rival team for World Series Cricket funded by Australian TV mogul Kerry Packer.
[69] But remain open to offers.

CHAPTER 5: DOUBLES, TWINS – AND IDENTITY

Even within the context of **Doctor Who,** which has had more than its fair share of doubles and twins over the years, *Black Orchid* does well to show as many variations on the theme as it does across the two episodes. There are the lookalikes, Nyssa and Ann Talbot. Then there is the Doctor and the Unknown becoming doubles of each other by using the same fancy dress costume. There are also two possible claimants to the name Lord Cranleigh, as discussed above. In addition the Doctor is, like Peter Wimsey in *Murder Must Advertise,* three different characters in the same story. He is himself, the identity he adopts in order to play cricket and also the Harlequin.

The idea of twins or lookalikes as plot elements has been part of literature for almost as long as people have been telling stories, and it is still used by both popular and literary writers. **Doctor Who** has explored the idea in numerous ways.

Several of the actors who have played the Doctor on screen have also played other parts. William Hartnell was also the Abbot of Amboise in *The Massacre.* Patrick Troughton played Salamander in *The Enemy of the World.* Colin Baker was Maxil in *Arc of Infinity* (1983) before he took over the part of the Doctor. Peter Capaldi was Caecilius in *The Fires of Pompeii* (2008), again, before going on to play the Doctor (and he was also John Frobisher in **Torchwood:** *Miracle Day* (2011), which is presumably canon as far as television **Doctor Who** is concerned).

While the 12th Doctor's resemblance to Caecilius eventually became a plot point in *The Girl Who Died* (2015), the Hartnell and Troughton cases are the most interesting, as the stories were written specifically for the Doctor to have a double, and in each case it is pivotal to the whole plot. On the most basic level, it gave the actors playing the part of the Doctor an opportunity to do something quite different while working on a series that was virtually a year-round job, and which made it difficult for either of them to take any other parts. Hartnell and Troughton were character actors able to play a variety of different roles. They are both good in the extra roles allotted to them, though we can only judge Hartnell on the basis of the soundtrack to *The Massacre*. In each case it works for the actor.

For the audience it works in terms of challenging our perceptions. Can we believe what we are seeing? Are we watching Hartnell as the Doctor pretending to be the Abbot or are we watching Hartnell as the Abbot? Are we watching Troughton as Salamander or Troughton as the Doctor pretending to be Salamander? Do we know more than the companions or other characters? In addition, seeing Hartnell and Troughton as totally different characters also highlights how they choose to play the Doctor. We understand and identify the nature of the Doctor more by seeing the actors resume the role. Similarly, when enemies of the Doctor take on his appearance in *Meglos* (1980) or *Arc of Infinity* (1983) it gives Tom Baker and Peter Davison, respectively, opportunities to play a villain impersonating the Doctor. Davison seems to have more fun with this rare opportunity to play a bad guy, something which Baker had done regularly in the years prior to taking the part of the Doctor.

David Tennant got to play dual roles of Time Lord Doctor and human Doctor in *Journey's End* (2010). Although this had the appearance of a plot direction taken to engineer a happy ending for Rose Tyler without affecting the ongoing format of the series, it opened potentially interesting opportunities for exploring the essence of what makes the Doctor the being he is.

As with the lead actors so also a similar pattern occurs with actors playing regular companions. Peter Purves, Nicholas Courtney, Ian Marter, Lalla Ward, Freema Agyeman and Karen Gillan (and Jenna Coleman, sort of) all played other characters before taking on their respective companion roles[70]. Jacqueline Hill went on to play a different part many years after leaving the series as a regular[71].

Obviously, this happens because producers and directors remember actors from something, and if they like their work they may choose to hire them again. In some cases the repeat casting becomes part of the story, as with Lalla Ward in the first episode of *Destiny of the Daleks* (1979) where it is clear that Romana is consciously basing her physical appearance on that of Princess Astra from *The Armageddon Factor* (1979).

The producers certainly got their money's worth out of Mary Tamm in *The Androids of Tara* where she plays four roles. As well as Romana, she plays Princess Strella and android doubles of each of those characters. The knockabout nature of the story means that

---

[70] In, respectively, 'Flight Through Eternity' (*The Chase* episode 3, 1965), *The Daleks' Master Plan*, *Carnival of Monsters* (1973), *The Armageddon Factor* (1979), *Army of Ghosts* (2006), *The Fires of Pompeii* and *Asylum of the Daleks* (2012).
[71] In *Meglos*.

little space is given to exploring the sense of identity of each one, but Tamm looks like she is enjoying herself.

There are other **Doctor Who** stories that at least match *Black Orchid* for doubles. *Inferno* (1970) has doubles of almost the whole cast. Only the Doctor, as an alien and outsider, is exempt. There are three dramatic purposes for the doubles in *Inferno*. One is to extend the story in an interesting way to last for the required seven episodes by developing a parallel world 'story within a story'. Then there is the idea of showing fascist versions of Lethbridge-Stewart and Liz Shaw. In each case the actors cleverly show us enough of the character we already know to show how unsettlingly close their counterpart is. The disturbing suggestion is that it doesn't take too much to make a fascist out of even those who we are used to seeing defending freedom. This in turn leads to the equally disturbing idea that it would not take much for any of us to fit into such a world. The third effect is to show us the real possibility that a world can be destroyed. After the Doctor returns to the main setting of the story, only he and the audience are aware of this. It heightens dramatic tensions and adds pathos.

The use of doubles is explored even more fully in *The Zygon Invasion / The Zygon Inversion* (2015). The Zygons are alien shapeshifters who can adopt the physical appearance of species with which they come into contact. Among the plethora of doubles thrown up by such a possibility is the character Osgood, played by Ingrid Oliver. Introduced in *The Day of the Doctor* (2013) and clearly written to become an instant fan favourite, Osgood had been killed by Missy in *Death in Heaven* (2014). However, in *The Zygon Invasion* we learn that Osgood was one of a large number of humans who had been replaced by Zygon doubles.

It is deliberately unclear whether the Osgood who died was the human or Zygon version (and there may be more than one Zygon version of course). The Doctor, and the viewers, really want Osgood to be alive. The inevitable question is asked at the end of *The Zygon Inversion*: is she the human Osgood or the Zygon Osgood? Her response is to dismiss the question. Osgood is Osgood. If she feels herself to be Osgood and has all the personality of Osgood then she is Osgood, regardless of whether or not she was originally Zygon or human.

There are problems with this. Firstly it exhibits a characteristic of the Zygons which was not evident before. The Zygons, as introduced in *Terror of the Zygons* (1975) showed no such tendency to symbiotically link themselves to a human double's very self[72]. Secondly the Zygons are clearly a sentient alien race. To assume they would be so willing to submerge their own personalities into another's identity is to devalue the being that the Zygon is. Either some aspect of the Zygon remains present, in which case Osgood is not truly Osgood, or the Zygons place no value on their own identities and are willing to sacrifice them with little concern, which would seem unlikely for a race which has expended much effort to travel across the galaxy to other planets. The Doctor is oddly unconcerned about this, given he thought it very much an issue

---

[72] An earlier attempt to use Zygons to explore identity in this way was attempted in the independent drama *Zygon* (aka *Zygon: When Being You Just Isn't Enough*) (2008), but the opportunity was partially lost in production problems. The original writers had their names removed from the credit and for marketing purposes the producer placed more emphasis on including nudity than on the drama.

when Amy and Clara were replaced by doubles[73]. Not only does he lack the concern of someone who was clearly fond of Osgood, but he lacks the curiosity of a scientist.

At the root of all this is the question of identity: what makes someone the person or being that they are? Do we require physical evidence of the person in the form of genes, DNA, physical material etc, before we can accept that someone is the person we believe them to be, or should we just be grateful that we can spend time with a personality we love even if it may be a construct of some kind? Given the Doctor's ability to change both his physical appearance and personality on a regular basis, perhaps he is just showing a different perspective on what has happened to Osgood. He may perceive differences in her case from those of Amy and Clara that make him less concerned. The viewer, if they were fond of Osgood as a character, may be grateful that she is still around to appear again, even if they are not fully convinced by the explanation for her being there. Those same viewers will likely claim that there is something essentially consistent about all incarnations of the Doctor: something in each case that they can put their finger on and say 'that's the Doctor'. (I've done it myself in this monograph when referring to, for example, the Doctor's quirkiness.) The audience looks for the Doctor to be the Doctor, even if the version played by Peter Capaldi has very little in common with the version played by William Hartnell.

That question of identity is raised in the very element of *Black Orchid* which so displeased Peter Davison: hiding his identity

---

[73] In *The Almost People* (2011) and *The Zygon Inversion* itself.

behind a mask. It is a brave or generous actor (or both) that is willing to remain undercover throughout – Hugo Weaving in *V for Vendetta* (2006) for example, or Karl Urban in *Dredd* (2012) (in contrast to Sylvester Stallone in *Judge Dredd* (1995)). Unlike Lord Peter Wimsey as Harlequin, the Doctor is unrecognisable. He could be anyone behind that mask. Once that visual identity is taken from him then the possibility is raised – for the other characters but not the viewer, as we are shown everything – that the Doctor could be guilty of murder. Being good at cricket does not eliminate him from suspicion and for Lady Cranleigh he is a useful stooge to whom otherwise awkward-to-explain murders can be attributed. Davison is right. Whether it is the script or the costume, the character of the Doctor is not pivotal in *Black Orchid*. It is more Nyssa's story than the Doctor's.

In a long-running series with a high episode count each year, that is not necessarily a problem. Starting with *Love and Monsters* (2006), **Doctor Who** has frequently included stories with reduced involvement for the Doctor. This is mainly to allow the lead actor some time off from a demanding role. Much dramatic television in the 21st century is based on having an ensemble cast. **Doctor Who** is one of a diminishing number of series that rely on a lead actor playing a lead character who is essential to much of what happens. This is not really sustainable in the long run. Nor is that a new phenomenon. Regular cast members were often written out for whole episodes in the first six series, when the lengths of the seasons were very long indeed (three-quarters of the year was not an unusual run). However, this is not the way the role of the Doctor is diminished here. Peter Davison is there throughout filming. He is not absent to allow him time off. It is just that the action is happening away from where he is much of the time. His role as the mysterious time-travelling figure who confronts the forces of evil wherever he finds them is put in question. His identity is less clear here than it has been since the difficult regeneration at the end of *Logopolis* (1981) and the beginning of *Castrovalva*.

Sarah Sutton joins the list of actors mentioned above who play companions to the Doctor as well as another character in the series. Like Mary Tamm in *The Androids of Tara* she plays two parts in the same story. Her twin roles of Nyssa and Ann Talbot allow Sutton more opportunities to express herself. While Davison is constrained by having to submerge his identity into the Harlequin, Sutton has the opportunity to develop Nyssa, to a limited extent, beyond what has gone before. Having been sidelined for the middle two episodes of *Kinda*, it is interesting that *Black Orchid* is the place where Nyssa once more comes to the fore. It would have been possible that having a double appear would detract from Nyssa as a character, in the way that the presence of the Doctor is reduced by having to share screen space with doubles in *The Massacre* or *The Enemy of the World*. In fact, the contrast between Nyssa and Ann gives some insights into who Nyssa is. Despite her physical resemblance, Ann is clearly a more experienced woman in some respects. She has been engaged twice, and even if both relationships have been chaste (about which the viewers can decide for themselves – there is no evidence in the script one way or the other) she must have acquired some insights into the world of adult relationships. Nyssa, up to this point in the series, has been portrayed as both young and previously protected from the outside world. It was only when the outside world, or universe, came to her that her stable life was challenged.

One of the more subtle things in *Black Orchid* is the way Adric is able to tell the difference between Nyssa and Ann. This is clearly deliberate on the part of Terence Dudley, and is one of the aspects of the story that he develops further in his novelisation:

> 'Poor Adric. It would only make matters worse if he attempted to explain to her that they'd been together long enough for him to be able to recognise certain of her little ways; her challenging stance, the set of her head when looking intently at anyone, the little intake of breath that preceded a sudden question.'[74]

Adric may be able to tell the difference but there are parts of *Black Orchid* where the viewers are not entirely sure. When Nyssa and Ann are in identical dresses and taking part in the dance, the viewer needs Adric to help us. By giving Nyssa a physical double the focus can be put on what makes her different; what her identity is. Unfortunately, what this mostly shows is how little the character of Nyssa has been developed since she was introduced in *The Keeper of Traken* (1981). She does at least get the chance to show in *Black Orchid* that she has a fun side. She is certainly up for the game of 'Guess who?' with Ann, she likes to dance and she likes the opportunity to wear more decorative clothes.

This is all enough to confuse George Cranleigh. Unlike Adric, he cannot tell the difference, nor is even aware most of the time that there are two people with the physical appearance of his beloved Ann. Where Adric has developed the experience and insight to be able to recognise the real Nyssa, George Cranleigh has lost his

---

[74] Dudley, *Black Orchid*, p55.

reason to such an extent that he cannot see beyond the physical appearance of what he expects Ann to look like. The person who is himself locked up because of what he looks like, in turn identifies Ann on the same basis.

The most pertinent double identity in *Black Orchid* is that of George Cranleigh. He is divided into the Cranleigh that once lived, explored the world, wrote books and loved Ann Talbot, and the Unknown. The tragedy of what he is resonates more fully once we know who he was and what happened to him. The Unknown, unable to be Cranleigh any more, takes the first alternative identity available to him: that of the Harlequin. In doing so he also masquerades as the Doctor. In whatever identity he takes on – Lord Cranleigh, the Unknown, the Harlequin, the Doctor – he fails in what he sets out to achieve. However, the love he clearly feels towards Ann Talbot remains ever-present. That love identifies George Cranleigh whatever he becomes or looks like. He retains that identity, at least. He is the man who never stopped loving his fiancée.

CHAPTER 6: THE HARLEQUIN

The Doctor and George Cranleigh have little in common in *Black Orchid,* except that they both wear, at different times, the Harlequin costume. The Doctor, in his fifth incarnation and especially in this story, is gregarious and friendly, while Cranleigh has lost the ability to communicate meaningfully with other human beings. The Doctor is the sum of his past experiences while Cranleigh is a shell of the person he formerly was. It is true that they are both outcasts, albeit in different ways, and that both are capable of being devious when it suits them. However, when each dons the costume of the Harlequin they are taking on an identity which reflects, in some way, aspects of themselves.

The Harlequin is an instantly recognisable yet constantly evolving character. The physical recognition comes from the distinctive chequered pattern costume of which we see an example in *Black Orchid*. Because the main feature of the costume is that patterning, it leaves open the option for an endless variety of designs. As shown in chapter one, the Harlequin can be seen with full face mask, half mask or no mask.

From origins in the Italian Commedia dell'arte performances, and possibly even earlier French passion plays, the Harlequin has been used as a character to do two main things. He, or more latterly she, is often part of a double act. Originally the Harlequin played off another physically identifiable character, the Pierrot. The Pierrot is usually shown in all white, save perhaps for a black skull cap. The face will usually be made up in white as well. The Pierrot is the straight man to the Harlequin and plots often involved him losing the woman he loves to the more dashing Harlequin. When the

Harlequin became adopted into British theatre, the double act evolved into the Harlequin and the Clown. The Clown is more clumsy and crude, while the Harlequin performs agile feats of acrobatics.

The other function of the Harlequin is to stir things up a bit. He is often the starting point of schemes and plots. Traditionally he is a servant who, sometimes subtly and sometimes obviously, undermines the plans of the master of the household. He also usually has his own romantic objectives. The Harlequin is no Fool. He will usually be portrayed as having wit and dexterity.

As time has gone by the Harlequin has acquired an aspect of the traditional trickster role in the way that he has been interpreted. He will become the random factor in a drama, as he does in *Black Orchid*.

The name alone was enough for Agatha Christie to make use of when she wrote her short stories about Mr Harley Quinn. She wanted a detective who would just be there when the plot required, and her readers accepted the character on that basis.

In science fiction, probably the most famous use of the Harlequin is in Harlan Ellison's short story '"Repent, Harlequin!", Said the Ticktockman'[75]. Ellison uses the Harlequin as a character who sets out deliberately to cause chaos in a society which is regulated to the point of sterility. The Harlequin here is an anarchist. No longer

---

[75] *Galaxy Magazine* (December 1965). The story is one of the more frequently anthologised short stories in the canon of American science fiction.

is he willing to settle for undermining his master; he wants to overthrow the whole system.

The Harlequin pattern has been used by dozens of sports teams. There are songs and albums by bands of a wide variety of types that have used the name.[76] There are publishing imprints[77]. Bernard Cornwell has used the name for a medieval knight in his novels[78], while Ian Watson appropriated it for one of his novels set in the **Warhammer 40K** far-future universe[79]. There is a medical condition called Harlequin's Syndrome. The word, the name, the idea, are very much part of our culture.

The highest profile use of the Harlequin concept in recent years is the DC Comics character Harley Quinn. Following in a tradition of characters dating back to the 1940s – all called Harlequin and all, interestingly, female – the modern Harley Quinn actually started as a character on television[80] before being incorporated into the DC comics from 1993. In the tradition of the double act, Quinn started out as a sidekick to the Joker before operating as a solo character

---

[76] For example, the album of the same name by Dave Grusin and Lee Ritenour (1985) and songs by Genesis (on the 1971 album *Nursery Cryme)* and The Hollies (on their 1979 album *Five Three One – Double Seven O Four*).

[77] Harlequin Romance is a recognised brand for romance fiction in North America since 1953. They own the British romance imprint, Mills & Boon, and are in turn owned by Harper Collins.

[78] Cornwell, Bernard, *Harlequin* (2000). This is the first in a series of four novels featuring the Harlequin.

[79] Watson, Ian, *Harlequin* (1990).

[80] **Batman: The Animated Series** (1992-95).

and, more recently, as part of a group in both the **Suicide Squad** comics and their 2016 film adaptation.

One aspect of the Harley Quinn comics character of particular note is her popularity with cosplayers — which appropriately brings the concept back, full circle, to its theatrical origins, but with the difference that Harley Quinn is now a female character while still fulfilling the dramatic purpose as a catalyst for chaos.

It is the harlequin costume in *Black Orchid* which enables George Cranleigh to do much of what he does. He certainly would not have got close to Ann were it not for the disguise. Cranleigh as Harlequin is, as the role traditionally would have it, in pursuit of his romantic objectives. He is also an agent of chaos in the well-ordered world of Cranleigh Hall. The Doctor as Harlequin does not pursue romantic interests or seek to undermine his hosts in any way. It is Cranleigh who is closer to the Harlequin type but in a way that is doomed to tragic failure. In this respect, rather than being part of a double act with either a Pierrot or Clown he is incorporating those roles into his own. He has the brutish clumsiness of the Clown and the romantic failure of the Pierrot added to his own Harlequin identity.

CHAPTER 7: STRUCTURE

One of the curiosities of *Black Orchid*, when first transmitted, was that it had only two episodes. As mentioned in the Introduction, this had happened only three times before in the series' history to that point. Of those three stories, the first two, despite their shorter running, time, place more emphasis on exploring the personalities of the principal cast members. *The Edge of Destruction* (1964) uses only the four regular cast members as characters; or five if we count the TARDIS, which plays a significant role in the action. Although the emotions of each character are heightened and twisted, this develops in such a way as to reveal something of the individual concerned, much as a bad drunk reveals something of their identity when they are not drunk. *The Rescue* (1965) shows us the compassionate side of the Doctor's personality, which had never really been evident in the first series. *The Sontaran Experiment*, by contrast, is a fast-paced adventure story. *Black Orchid*, in not having the by-then-traditional four episodes to play out a full science fiction thriller, chooses instead to take more of its time to allow the four time travellers to play and party and socialise.

Black Orchid also started a short-running tradition. Each of the two subsequent seasons contained a two-part story among other stories which were all four parts[81]. *The King's Demons* (1983) was again written by Terence Dudley – who, if we also take into account

---

[81] I count *Resurrection of the Daleks* as four-part story for these purposes, as that is how it was produced, even though it was initially shown in two longer episodes to fit into schedules altered to accommodate coverage of the 1984 Winter Olympics.

K-9 and Company: *A Girl's Best Friend*, made something of a specialism of writing for a shorter length. Three of his four stories run to less than 50 minutes. After *The Awakening* the two-part stories (at least of 25 minutes' length per part) fell out of favour again. In production terms *The Ultimate Foe* (1986) is a two-part story but in narrative terms it only makes sense (if indeed it does make sense) in the context of being the final two episodes of the 14-part story *The Trial of a Time Lord* (1986). What *The King's Demons* and *The Awakening* (and *The Ultimate Foe*) have in common is a faster pace than *Black Orchid*. They also make excellent use of their filming locations. Like *Black Orchid, The Awakening* was originally pitched as a four-parter but commissioned as a two-parter.

After 1986 the series made regular use of three-part stories. In doing so the production team were moving in the direction of telling what would previously have been four-part stories at a brisker pace. It also allowed the standard three-act play structure that underpins many narratives to be accommodated more naturally into the episode format.

Since the broadcast of *Rose* in 2005, the most commonly used episode structure has been single 45-minute (approximately) episodes. There have been frequent two-part stories and some longer single episodes, but the 45-minute length is the default. This reflects changing patterns in making, viewing and marketing television drama. When **Doctor Who** started in 1963, half-hour drama series were quite common, whether in the form of action series like **Danger Man** (1960-1962, 1964-1966), more contemporary drama such as **Z Cars**[82] (1962-1978), or serials like the classic serials strand which the BBC moved from Saturday evening to Sunday evening to make room for **Doctor Who.** Even by 1982 the idea of half-hour drama was unusual unless it was an ongoing soap. When **Doctor Who** was moved to weekday evenings in 1982 it was placed in the schedules where, at other times of the year, viewers would be watching **Angels** (1975-83), a hospital-based soap, or **Triangle** (1981-1983), a bizarre soap set in the glamorous world of ferries travelling to and from mainland Europe. By 2005 the only drama series that used the half-hour episode format were either soaps or drama series made specifically for children. In order to be taken seriously and in order to be sold around the world, the 45-minute episode was inevitable.

Black Orchid was not ahead of its time in telling a complete **Doctor Who** story in about 45 minutes. It would be nonsense to suggest that Russell T Davies was inspired by *Black Orchid,* when looking for a format for the series as broadcast from 2005. The pacing and content are vastly different. Compare *Black Orchid* with *The Unicorn and the Wasp* (2008), and it becomes clear how much faster-moving the latter is. There is time for a whodunit and a monster story as well as some nice character asides. *Black Orchid* takes 30 minutes to get to the point reached by *The Unicorn and the Wasp* after about five. What has happened is that stories that would have unfolded over four episodes in the 1970s, and might have been told in three in the 1980s, are now likely to be told in a single 45-minute episode.

---

[82] Both of which evolved into 50-minute episodes.

And yet, isn't it a bit of a pleasure to go back to this little two-part story, every now and again, and see the Doctor enjoying a game of cricket, Nyssa learning to dance and Tegan, for once, enjoying everything. And Adric gets to eat to excess and dance with pretty girls before... well, before.

APPENDIX 1: IS *BLACK ORCHID* A TRUE HISTORICAL?

Conventional wisdom among historians of **Doctor Who** will say that in the 1960s the series contained a number of stories best described as 'historical' stories. Sometimes, to differentiate them from stories such as *The Time Meddler* (1965), (which was a science fiction story which happened to have, or required, a historical setting), they are described as 'pure historicals' or 'straight historicals'. There were 10 in all[83], but after *The Highlanders* no more were made. Instead, when the Doctor ventured into Earth history he did so following the template established by *The Time Meddler*, and the historical setting was a backdrop for a science fiction story such as *The Time Warrior* (1973-1974) or *The Masque of Mandragora* (1976). *Black Orchid* followed just such a story, *The Visitation*, in the 1982 season.

Those 10 historical stories do not all fall into the same pattern. The most common type involved the Doctor and his companions interacting with significant historical people and events: the template for this was established with *Marco Polo* and continued in the likes of *The Romans* and *The Crusade*. Then there are the ones where the historical setting is a genre in itself: *The Smugglers* is a pirate adventure more than a historical story. Then there is the

---

[83] *Marco Polo, The Aztecs* (1964), *The Reign of Terror, The Romans, The Crusade* (1965), *The Myth Makers* (1965), *The Massacre, The Gunfighters, The Smugglers* (1966) and *The Highlanders*. Of these, *The Myth Makers* is, as the title says, rooted more in legendary fiction than history. All of them are adventure fiction first and history second.

type which uses the historical context to question the very idea of time travel: in *The Aztecs* Barbara faces the dilemma of whether she can or should try to change history. The story relies on her knowledge of the future in a way that is never central to *Marco Polo* or *The Smugglers*. But which of these templates, if any, does *Black Orchid* try to follow?

Black Orchid was designed to be a return to the straight historical story[84]. The 'monster' would be one of natural causes and explanation. The Doctor and his companions would have an adventure in the time period of the story without any science fictional elements. However, in the second episode, the Doctor uses the TARDIS to travel back to the country house. He also takes passengers from the time period. There is then a science fiction element which does intrude into the story.

Which is curious, really, as it doesn't need to be there. It would have been simple to write the script so that the Doctor and his companions raced back to the house in one of the splendid vintage cars. Indeed it might have added dramatic impetus if the viewer watched to see how close to causing further deaths George Cranleigh might go before the Doctor could arrive in time to save the day. Perhaps the budget of the show restricted the amount of filming time available with the cars. Maybe Terence Dudley, or script editor Eric Saward, just preferred to do it the way it stands. It does allow the Doctor to take control for the first time since the cricket match finished, but, again, that could have been achieved equally well by letting Davison take the wheel of the speeding car.

---

[84] Pixley, 'Fact File'.

The use of the TARDIS serves no real purpose in driving the plot forward or developing any of the characters.

Black Orchid, then, is not strictly speaking a true historical story but it is in intention and spirit. Despite the intrusion of the TARDIS it is not really trying to explore a science fictional concept. It is closer to the format established in *The Smugglers* and *The Highlanders* where all the characters are new fictional creations following recognisable period archetypes.

There are good reasons for adopting each of the three templates identified above. The model chose by *Black Orchid* allows the writer to tell any type of story he wants. It also allows them to use the audience's knowledge and familiarity with the setting. Terence Dudley does not, as represented in the final version, make full use of those opportunities in terms of telling a truly original story but he does use the audience's ability to do some of the work because they know about dramas set in 1920s country houses. However, it did not make enough of a mark to reinvigorate the sub-genre. Those wanting to see **Doctor Who** do more stories set in Earth history without any further SF elements beyond the presence of the Doctor and his companions would have to look to other media, where a number of novels and audio productions have successfully utilised the form.

APPENDIX 2: THE CRANLEIGH FAMILY LEGACY

One of the pleasant surprises in *Black Orchid* is that the Doctor and his companions do not jump into the TARDIS the second the plot has been resolved but instead stay around to attend the funeral of George Cranleigh. It is a surprise, both because it is not something the Doctor has previously ever shown any inclination to do and also because it uses some of the screen time for something which is not essential to the plot. However, the latter point is hardly unique in *Black Orchid*.

It is pleasant to see it happen, because it shows that the Doctor has been affected by the events of the story. Despite the slight nature of the actual plot, the real point here is the human tragedy of George Cranleigh, and it is that to which the Doctor is responding by attending the funeral. For a series which has never been squeamish about writing out regular cast members offscreen[85], or dismissing them with seemingly little concern[86], this attention to detail is noteworthy.

One of the differences between the fan and the casual viewer is that the fan will, ten years after we last saw Jo Grant, still be wondering what happened to her. The Cranleigh family have not, as yet, returned to **Doctor Who** on television but they have featured in some of the original novels.

---

[85] Liz Shaw (at some point between *Inferno* and *Terror of the Autons* (1971), Peri (at some point during *The Trial of a Time Lord* (1986)).
[86] Dodo (at some point in *The War Machines*).

In *The Sands of Time* by Justin Richards (1996) the Doctor returns to Cranleigh Hall in 1926, one year after the events of *Black Orchid*. He is there to attend the wedding reception of Charles Cranleigh and Ann Talbot. He also gets to meet Smutty Thomas, who is portrayed as a drunk[87]. It is a brief vignette in the novel but significant, especially as a later scene more pivotal to the plot also shows Ann, Lady Cranleigh, in old age[88].

Paul Cornell's *Goth Opera* refers to the Doctor having written an article for *Wisden*[89] about charity cricket games played in legacy and commemoration of Lord Cranleigh. The article is entitled 'By Lord Cranleigh's Invitation, Seventy Years of Charity Elevens'[90]. Presumably Lord Cranleigh's XI bears some similarity to organisations like the Lords Taverners.

Daniel O'Mahony's *Falls the Shadow* (1994) features a 21st-century character named Justin Cranleigh, who another character speculates may be related to the eminent botanist[91]. Like his possible forebear, Justin wears a mask to cover a facial disfigurement and is dangerously insane.

Combined with the book *Black Orchid*, which George Cranleigh is shown to have written, the fictional legacy of the Cranleigh family is already established. **Doctor Who** being what it is, that may yet be added to further.

---

[87] Richards, Justin, *The Sands of Time*, pp7-9.
[88] Richards, *The Sands of Time*, p287.
[89] The recognised authoritative record for cricket, published annually.
[90] Cornell, *Goth Opera*, p25.
[91] O'Mahony, Daniel, *Falls the Shadow*, p333.

APPENDIX 3: 'THE WATCHER' ON *BLACK ORCHID*

Like the Doctor I tend to side with the underdog in most things. It's a rare occasion when I've voted for a winning candidate in any election. I hope I've made a case in the main monograph for why *Black Orchid* is worth our attention. In this respect I am as one with the Watcher, columnist of note in *Doctor Who Magazine,* who has come back to examine this story three times in the first 63 instalments of 'A History of Doctor Who in 100 Objects'. Given there are well over 200 **Doctor Who** stories to choose from, that is an allocation almost as generous as the screen time given to the cricket match in *Black Orchid*.

For the most part the Watcher mercilessly, and accurately, dismantles whole sections of the plot of *Black Orchid*. On the question of the Cranleigh family tree[92] I will challenge the argument put forward. How can Charles Cranleigh be Lord Cranleigh if George Cranleigh is still alive? Why would his book on the black orchid be credited as by George Cranleigh if he was actually Lord Cranleigh? One option offered up by the Watcher, that George Cranleigh rejected his peerage, doesn't work for two reasons. First, that was not a legal option until 1963. Secondly, where titles are rejected they remain dormant until the person who has rejected it dies, at which point the next in line inherits said title. The example of Tony Benn illustrates this. From 1963 until his death in 2014 there was

---

[92] 'The Watcher', 'A History of Doctor Who in 100 Objects #60: The Cranleigh Family Tree', DWM #489.

no Viscount Stansgate. Once Benn died his elder son, Stephen, became the third Viscount.

The Watcher is on the right lines to look in the direction of Lady 'stone-cold bitch' Cranleigh. She must have had George Cranleigh declared legally dead despite knowing he is alive – another good reason for keeping the man locked away and out of sight. Did money change hands to 'arrange' things in Venezuela? Is Dudley suggesting that such corruption is easy to arrange in those funny far-off places?

Even if George Cranleigh was legally Lord Cranleigh it does not follow that he would use his title on his academic writings. Bertrand Russell never used 'Earl Russell' as the author credit on any of his books. Ah, but he was a socialist. How about the Conservative John Buchan? Do we think of his books as written by Baron Tweedsmuir?

In the case of Tegan's improbable knowledge of George Cranleigh's writings,[93] the Watcher is on target. It is possible that Tegan might have heard of Cranleigh as botanist while not being aware of the Fancy Dress Murders of 1925. Sometimes such scandals are forgotten – see, for example, the case of Edward Bulwer-Lytton mentioned earlier. There are more people who have heard of Bulwer-Lytton the writer than know that he outraged society by trying to have his perfectly sound but estranged wife locked up as insane. If you want a murder case, how many people remember the founding family of ICI, the Brunners, for the spousal murder

---

[93] 'The Watcher', 'A History of Doctor Who in 100 Objects #43: Tegan's Screwdriver', DWM #472.

and accompanying suicide of 1927[94]? So, possible, but not terribly likely. I'm actually more sceptical of Tegan having heard of Cranleigh the botanist than that she might not have heard of the murders.

The Watcher makes a case for Lord Cranleigh being a bit of a 'thicko'[95]. The evidence is overwhelming, but doesn't Michael Cochrane do it well?

No one, least of all me, is going to claim that *Black Orchid* is a great story. It has many flaws and faults but they are interesting flaws and faults.

It seems to be appropriate to give the last word on *Black Orchid* to the Watcher, who occupies the last page of written content in DWM:

> 'It's remarkable how many layers of interest and intrigue lurk in the crinkles of Terence Dudley's bottomlessly fascinating two-parter.'

---

[94] Bevan R.M., *Formula for Murder: The I.C.I. Mystery*
[95] 'The Watcher', 'A History of Doctor Who in 100 Objects #63: Lord Cranleigh's Brain', DWM #492.

BIBLIOGRAPHY

Books

Adams, Douglas, *Life, the Universe and Everything*. 1982. London, Pan, 2009. ISBN 9780330508575.

Asimov, Isaac, ed, *The Hugo Winners 1963-1967*. London, Sphere, 1973.

Bevan, RM, *Formula for Murder: The ICI Mystery*. Chester, CC publishing, 2003. ISBN 094900121X.

Bronte, Anne, *The Tenant of Wildfell Hall*. 1848. London, Penguin, 1979. ISBN 9780140431377.

Bronte, Charlotte, *Jane Eyre*. 1847. London, Penguin, 1996. ISBN 9780140434002.

Burnett, Frances Hodgson, *The Secret Garden*. 1911. London, Vintage, 2012. ISBN 9780099572954.

Collins, Wilkie, *The Woman in White*. 1859. London, Penguin, 1994. ISBN 9780140620245.

Cooray Smith, James, *The Massacre*. **The Black Archive** #2. Edinburgh, Obverse Books, 2016. ISBN 9781909031388.

Cornell, Paul, *Goth Opera*. **Doctor Who: The Missing Adventures**. London, Virgin Publishing Ltd, 1994. ISBN 9780426204183.

Dudley, Terence, *Black Orchid*. **The Target Doctor Who Library** #113. London, WH Allen, 1986. ISBN 0426202546.

Friedrich, Gary, and Doug Moench, *Essential Monster of Frankenstein*. New York, Marvel, 2004. ISBN 9780785116349.

Hamilton, Duncan, *Harold Larwood*. London, riverrun, 2009. ISBN 9781847249494.

Howe, David J, and Stephen James Walker, *Doctor Who: The Television Companion*. London, BBC Books, 1998. ISBN 9780563405887.

Howe, David J, Mark Stammers and Stephen James Walker, *Doctor Who: The Eighties*. London, Virgin Publishing, 1997. ISBN 9780753501283.

Hugo, Victor, *Notre-Dame de Paris*. 1831. London, Penguin, 2004. John Sturrock, trans, ISBN 9780140443530.

Leroux, Gaston, *The Phantom of the Opera*. Mireille Ribiere, trans, London, Penguin, 2012. ISBN 9780141191508.

Lycett, Andrew, *Wilkie Collins: A Life of Sensation*. London, Windmill Books, 2014. ISBN 9780099557340.

Matheson, Richard, *The Shrinking Man*. 1955. **SF Masterworks.** London, Gollancz, 2014. ISBN 9781473201699.

Miles, Lawrence, and Tat Wood, *198-1984: Seasons 18 to 21*. **About Time: The Unauthorized Guide to Doctor Who** #5. Des Moines, Mad Norwegian Press, 2005. ISBN 9780975944646.

Myles, LM, *The Ambassadors of Death*. **The Black Archive** #3. Edinburgh, Obverse Books, 2016. ISBN 9781909031395.

O'Mahony, Daniel, *Falls the Shadow*. **Doctor Who: The New Adventures**. London, Virgin Publishing Ltd, 1994. ISBN 9780426204275.

Polidori, John, 'The Vampyre: A Tale'. New Monthly Magazine. April 1819.

Richards, Justin, *The Sands of Time*. 1996. **The Monster Collection**. London, BBC Books, 2014. ISBN 9781849907675.

Rhys, Jean, *Wide Sargasso Sea*. 1966. London, Penguin Books, 1997. ISBN 9780141182858.

Scoones, Paul, *The Comic Strip Companion: The Unofficial Guide to Doctor Who in Comics: 1964-1979*. Prestatyn, Telos Publishing Ltd, 2012. ISBN 9781845830700.

Sayers, Dorothy L, *Murder Must Advertise*. 1933. London, Hodder, 1983. ISBN 9780450002427.

Shelley, Mary, *Frankenstein, Or The Modern Prometheus*. 1818 revised 1831. Penguin Books, 2003. ISBN 9780141439471.

Simpson, MJ, *Hitchhiker: A Biography of Douglas Adams*. London, Hodder, 2003. ISBN 9780340824894.

Tomlinson, Richard, *Amazing Grace: The Man Who Was WG*. London, Little Brown, 2015. ISBN 9781408705179

Trollope, Anthony, *He Knew He Was Right*. 1859. London, Penguin, 1994. ISBN 9781040433913

Walker, Stephen James, ed, *Volume Three: The Eighties*. ***Talkback: The Unofficial and Unauthorised Doctor Who Interview Book***. Tolworth, Telos Publishing Ltd, 2007. ISBN 9781845830144.

Wood, Ellen, *East Lynne*. 1861. Oxford, OUP, 2008. ISBN 9780199536030.

Periodicals

Doctor Who Magazine (DWM). Marvel UK, Panini, BBC, 1979-.

Review , DWM #65, cover date June 1982.

Briggs, Nick, 'Peter Davison – Dr Moo?' part 2, DWM #214, cover date 6 July 1994.

Cornell, Paul, 'Black Orchid: Someone Somewhere (in Summertime)'. DWM Special Edition #1: *The Complete Fifth Doctor*, cover date March 2002.

Cook, Benjamin, 'The DWM Interview'. DWM #500, cover date July 2016.

Furman, Simon, 'Nature of the Beast!' part 1. DWM #111, cover date April 1986.

Gillatt, Gary, 'Black Orchid' (DVD review). DWM #395, cover date May 2008.

Pixley, Andrew, 'Fact File'. *Doctor Who Magazine 10th Anniversary Special Issue*, October 1989.

'The Watcher', 'A History of Doctor Who in 100 Objects #43: Tegan's Screwdriver'. DWM #472, cover date May 2014.

'The Watcher', 'A History of Doctor Who in 100 Objects #60: The Cranleigh Family Tree'. DWM #489, cover date September 2015.

'The Watcher', 'A History of Doctor Who in 100 Objects #63: Lord Cranleigh's Brain', DWM #492, cover date December 2015.

Doctor Who Classic Comics. Marvel UK, Panini, 1992-94.

Doctor Who: The Forgotten. IDW, 2008.

#3, October 2008.

Dracula Lives. Marvel UK, 1974-76.

Galaxy. World Editions, Galaxy Publishing, Universal Publishing, 1950-1980.

The Monster of Frankenstein / The Frankenstein Monster. Marvel Comics, 1973-75.

Radio Times. BBC Magazines, Immediate Media Company 1921-.

Richardson, David, 'Friend or Foe? *Black Orchid* Reviewed'. *Skaro* vol 2 #5, June 1982.

Shiver and Shake. IPC, 1974-75.

TV Comic. News of the World, Beaverbrook Newspapers, TV Publications, Polystyle Publications, 1951-84.

'Egyptian Escapade', *TV Comic* #820, 2 September 1967.

Television

All Creatures Great and Small. BBC, 1978-90.

Batman: The Animated Series. Warner Brothers Television, 1992-95

Colditz. BBC, Universal Television, 1972-74.

Columbo. NBC, Universal, 1971-78, 1989-2003.

Doctor Who. BBC, 1963-.

Danger Man. ITC, 1960-61, 1964-66.

Doomwatch. BBC, 1970-1972.

Frankenstein: The True Story. Universal/NBC, 1973.

Jane Eyre. BBC, 1973.

Jane Eyre. BBC, 1983.

K-9 and Company. BBC, 1981.

A Girl's Best Friend.

The Man from U.N.C.L.E. Arena Productions, MGM, NBC, 1964-68.

Murder Must Advertise. BBC, 1973.

The Seven Dials Mystery. London Weekend Television, 1981.

Survivors. BBC, 1975-77.

The Tomorrow People. Thames Television, ITV, 1973-79

Torchwood. BBC Wales, BBC Worldwide, Canadian Broadcasting Corporation, Starz Entertainment, 2006-11.

Children of Earth. Five episodes, 2009.

Wings. BBC, 1977-1978.

Why Didn't They Ask Evans? London Weekend Television, 1980.

Z Cars. BBC, 1962-1978.

Film

Arnold, Jack, dir, *The Incredible Shrinking Man*. Universal, 1957

Asquith, Anthony, dir, *The Final Test*. ACT Films Limited, 1953.

Barton, Charles, dir, *Abbott and Costello Meet Frankenstein*. Universal International Pictures, 1948.

Clair, Rene, dir, *And Then There Were None.* Rene Clair Productions, 1945.

Hamilton, Guy, dir, *Live and Let Die*. Eon Productions, 1973.

Julian, Rupert, dir, *The Phantom of the Opera*. Universal Pictures, 1925.

LeRoy, Mervyn, dir, *Quo Vadis*. Metro-Goldwyn-Meyer, 1951.

Lumet, Sidney, dir, *Murder on the Orient Express*. EMI, 1974.

Mann, Delbert, dir, *Jane Eyre*. Omnibus Productions/NBC, 1970.

Sitch, Rob, dir, *The Dish*. Working Dog, 2000.

Stevenson, Robert, dir, *Jane Eyre*. 20th Century Fox, 1943.

Sturges, John, dir, *Gunfight at the OK Corral*. Metro-Goldwyn-Meyer, 1957.

Whale, James, dir, *Frankenstein*. Universal Pictures, 1931.

Wilder, Billy, dir, *Witness for the Prosecution*. Metro-Goldwyn-Meyer, 1957.

Worsley, Wallace, dir, *The Hunchback of Notre Dame*. Universal Pictures, 1923.

Radio

Test Match Special. BBC, 1957-.

Websites

'BBC Genome Project'. http://genome.ch.bbc.co.uk/. Accessed 23 July 2016.

Sullivan, Shannon Patrick, 'Doctor Who: The Lost Stories'. http://www.shannonsullivan.com/drwho/lost.html. Accessed 23 July 2016.

BIOGRAPHY

Ian Millsted writes on comics for *Back Issue, Comic Book Creator* and *Alter Ego*. He has contributed essays to *You and Who Else* and *You on Target*. He has contributed short stories to the anthologies *Airship Shape and Bristol Fashion, North by Southwest* and a new Professor Challenger story for *Challenger Unbound*. His western novella *Silence Rides Alone* was published by Sundown Press in 2016. He lives in Bristol with his wife and daughter.